SECRETS of
MODERN
SLOT
PLAYING

L&M Publications
1118 W. Magnolia Blvd., #203
Burbank, CA 91506

Phone or Fax (818) 569-0208   E-mail: larrymak@playful.com

3rd Edition
January 2001

Author's Note

Slot technology and casino policies change fast. Although every attempt has been made to ensure the accuracy of the information in this book, some specific references may become outdated as time goes by. Fortunately, this will not affect the basic information you need to be a knowledgeable slot player. Good Luck!

Larry Mak

Printed in the United States of America

ISBN 0-9664592-0-2
Library of Congress Catalog Card Number 99-97167

Graphics by Beachwood Graphics
Edited by Nelson Carter (cncarter@writeme.com)

CONTENTS

SUGGESTED PLAYING STRATEGIES

ETCETERA

CASINO COMEDY

*A **woman was watching** her boyfriend play roulette at an Atlantic City casino. He handed her a $5 chip and told her to bet one of the numbers.*

"Which one should I play?" she asked.

"Oh, just bet it on your age," he said. She placed the chip on number 25. The roulette ball landed on 32 — and the woman fainted.

*At **one of those** family-oriented casinos in Las Vegas, a 7-year old asked her mother, "Mommy, where are the SOB slots?"*

The mother thought a moment, then said, "Oh, they just bring those out when daddy plays."

***Wife to husband:** "Dear, I saved $50 by not playing the quarter slots this morning."*

"That's good," the husband replied. "But you could have saved more by not playing the dollar slots."

***One of the amenities** featured in the Paris-Las Vegas casino resort is a cocktail bar called Chez When.*

***English Teacher:** "Name three collective nouns."*
***Student:** "Flypaper, wastepaper basket, slot machine."*

***He:** "Do you really believe there's intelligent life on Mars?*
***She:** "Of course. You don't see them throwing money away on casinos, do you?"*

*A **reporter asked the** manager of a Las Vegas casino whether there was any truth to the rumor that organized crime still had a hand in casino operations.*

"Why, that's ridiculous!" exclaimed the manager. Then turning to an associate, said, "Isn't it, Little Louie?"

***After a long playing** session, my wife loves to go shopping. Last week in a casino mall in Reno, she paid an outrageous $750 for a clock from the Black Forest in Germany. And what a clock. At home, a little bird comes out of the clock every hour and describes her.*

SECRETS OF MODERN SLOT PLAYING

Here it is: A new, fun-filled, Las Vegas-tested guide to today's casinos and their high-tech computerized slots.

In just minutes you'll learn:

* What slots to play and how to play them.

* The most common mistakes slot players make and how to avoid them.

* Simple tips and tricks you can apply in any casino anywhere.

* How today's slots work and why they're so hard to beat.

> **NOTE:** The suggested slot-playing strategies in this book are designed for the straight, three-reel slots with fixed payout schedules. Multiline, multicoin slots and specialty games like video poker and video blackjack are not included.

****

Dear Fellow Slot Player:

If you are an average slot player with a limited bankroll who plays mostly for the fun of gambling and (hopefully) winning, this book is for you.

It contains up-to-the-minute tips and techniques passed along by casino insiders, mathematicians, programmers, computer scientists, and slot-wise players nationwide. Plus the author's more than 30 years' experience playing slots at the major gaming meccas across the country.

You'll learn everything you need to know about today's high-tech computerized slots: what to do, how to do it, and why you're doing it. Plus, you'll have fun along the way.

To be quite honest, this book won't show you how to "beat the slots." No book can do that. But it will show you how to keep your losses down and how to extend your bankroll and playing time. The true secret of slot playing is to s-t-r-e-t-c-h your money over time. The longer you can make your money and playing time last, the better chance you have of hitting a hot streak or a big jackpot.

About slot odds and probability. All you need to know about odds is that they're high and they're against you. All you need to know about probability is that the longer you play, the greater the probability you'll lose. They don't build those ritzy megaresorts and cruise-to-nowhere riverboats on winners!

Some players ask, "Does it really help to play with a 'winning' attitude?" Quite frankly...**no!** Slot players are among the most superstitious people in the world. And this is one of their most cherished beliefs.

In reality, a "winning attitude" is nothing but a wishful-thinking fantasy. A mental four-leaf clover or rabbit's foot. It's OK to believe in a "winning attitude" as long as you know it's just part of the game — not something to take seriously.

Today's slot machine is really a computer in slot's clothing. And a player's attitude has no effect whatsoever on the tiny computer chip that randomly determines the game's outcome. To believe otherwise is sheer superstition.

Perhaps the best attitude to have is to be optimistic but realistic. That is, be confident, expect to win. But be realistic about your chances.

~~~~~~~~~~~~~~~*The Positive Attitude*~~~~~~~~~~~~~~~~~
Joe: "I'm going to Las Vegas tomorrow. Got $600 to lose."
Bill: "Don't talk like that! You should never take a negative approach to gambling. Always think positive."
Joe: "OK. I'm positive I'm going to lose $600."
~~~~~~

"Winning at slots is pure luck," says Steve Wynn, chairman of Mirage Resorts. Still, there are a few things you can do to help luck along and make your slot playing a more fun-filled, exciting experience. Just follow the simple, common-sense tips and guidelines in this book. If you do, you'll be on your way to becoming a smart player and not just another slot player.

1
HOW TODAY'S SLOTS WORK

Ignorance may be bliss, but not when it comes to slots. What you don't know can hurt you — and your wallet. To have any hope of winning, you must have some idea of how today's high-tech computerized slots work. And below, is your personal computer tutor. It tells in plain, nontechnical language all that you really need to know.

Today's slots are controlled by a miniature computer (microprocessor) that generates random win-loss symbol combinations nonstop, 24 hours a day, 7 days a week, whether the slot is being played or not.

With most of today's slots, no matter how many coins you put in, the computer selects a win-loss symbol combination the instant you pull the handle or press the "spin" button. The computer then sends an electronic signal to the reel motors telling them to spin the reels and display the win-loss symbol combination it has chosen for you.

This is the only function the reels serve. They have no effect on the outcome.

And since the computer's choice of win-loss symbol combinations is 100% random, no one can predict what symbols will appear and when. A common misconception is that because there are fewer players, the wee hours of the morning (12:00 to 5:00 a.m.) and the so-called "off-hours" (6:00 p.m. to 8:00 p.m.) are the best times to play. But given the randomness factor of the slot's computer program, *there is no one day of the week or part of the day or night that is better to play than any other!*

3

THE RANDOM NUMBER GENERATOR

Here's a closer look at the slot's computer program for the more technically minded reader.

Today's slots are controlled by a microprocessor, which is a fancy name for a computer and some associated memory on a silicon chip. Built into the memory is a program that assigns a series of numbers to all possible symbols on the reel strip. Here, each bar, each cherry, each blank is assigned a series of numbers. The more numbers assigned to a particular symbol or blank, the more often that result will appear.

Another part of the program is called the Random Number Generator (RNG). The instant you pull the handle or press the button, the RNG selects three numbers and signals the reels to display the three symbols which correspond to the three numbers. For example, numbers **7-34-22** may be displayed as **cherry-cherry-cherry**.

There are tons of numbers causing the reels to stop at blank-blank-blank, but only a few that cause the reels to stop at **7-7-7**.

This number selection also determines the machine's percentage payback. The more numbers assigned to winning symbols, the higher the slot's percentage payback.

In a second version of the RNG, just one number is assigned to each possible reel result. For example, 772 may result in a display of bar-bar-cherry. Which version of the RNG a manufacturer uses is proprietary information and is a big secret.

When do you stop the RNG? That depends on the manufacturer. One may program the RNG to stop when the handle is pulled or the button is pushed. Another may have the RNG stop when the first coin is inserted. There's no way to tell.

So it's the RNG that really decides whether you win or lose. It doesn't care how many coins you put in, the time of day or night, whether you pull the handle or press the button, or stand on your head.

CAUTION! SLOT SYSTEM SCAMS

Beware of ads in newspapers, magazines, mail order flyers or on e-mail or the Internet hawking some type of "secret" or "sure-fire" system for beating the slots. The ad usually has some type of eye-catching headline like:

Slot Mechanic Reveals Secrets of Slots!
or
How I Robbed the One-Armed Bandits, Legally

These "systems" are merely attempts by slot quacks and charlatans to cash in on the universal dream of every slot player — a magic formula for beating the unbeatable.

The offer usually states that it's limited. And comes with a money-back, no-questions-asked guarantee if not satisfied. A real win-win situation for the vendor. For only 2-3% of dissatisfied customers ever bother to return unwanted material. Most are too embarrassed to admit they've been ripped off.

Some vendors may not ask questions. But they stipulate that the material returned be in a reusable, resalable condition. And guess, folks, who determines that!

One huckster described himself as a disgruntled ex-casino employee who just wanted to get back at the casino. Another simply said he was no longer interested in money. But what you get doesn't live up to the win-big promise implied by the title.

The material is often poorly written and cheaply bound. Some are worthless, out of date, or out-and-out scams. And expensive ones at that ($20 to $500)! Just ask yourself: If you discovered a way to make tax-free millions playing the slots, would you sell it for a few dollars? Of course not! Say to yourself:

There is NO system! There is NO system! There is NO system!

— Riddle —

Under what sign of the Zodiac were all those "sure-fire" slot systems born?

Answer : ♉ *(Taurus)*

5

1. Percentage Payback. By state law, each slot machine is required to return a certain percentage of all the money put into it (payback) and keep the rest as profit (hold). The hold varies from machine to machine and casino to casino.

In Nevada, one machine might pay back 97%, while the one right next to it pays a whopping low 80%!

In New Jersey, the minimum required payback is 83%. In Nevada, it's 75%. But throughout the country, the average percentage payback is somewhere between 85% and 95%.

A slot's percentage payback is programmed into a computer chip by the manufacturer. When a casino orders a particular model slot from the manufacturer, it specifies the percentage payback it wants the slot to have — from a low 75% (horrible!) to a high 98% (terrific!).

A slot with a high percentage payback is called "loose." One with a low percentage payback is called "tight."

You'll generally find looser slots in gaming areas where there's a lot of competition. Slots in areas with just one or two isolated casinos tend to be tighter.

> NOTE: Always play the highest denomination slot you can comfortably afford to play. A look at the Casino Player's Slot Chart on the following pages will show that the higher the denomination slot, the higher the percentage payback (shown as **WIN** %). The one- or two-point spread doesn't look like much, but each added percentage point increases your chances of winning.

Theoretically, a slot with an advertised payback of 92% will return $92 of every $100 put into it and keep $8 as profit. But the 92% is just a long-term average — meaning that the slot is programmed to pay back 92% of all coins played. Not just to one player, but to *all* its players (hundreds, maybe thousands). And in no set period of time. Just eventually.

So, for example, if you were to drop $100 into a slot with a known 92% payback, you wouldn't get back exactly $92 in the time you were at that slot. You might get more, less, or nothing at all.

It may also come as a shock to learn that you can still lose a bundle even on slots with an advertised payback of 98% or 99%! The casino edge of 1% or 2% may not sound like much, but it applies to every bet you make. And over time it eats away your bankroll.

PS: Don't bother asking slot floor personnel what a slot's payback percentage is. They won't know.

2."Up to 97.4% Payback." Some major casinos set aside a carousel area (mostly dollar slots) with a large overhead sign touting "Up to 97.4% payback." Notice the "Up to."

The sign is somewhat misleading. It fails to mention that there may be only one of these higher-payback slots in that area, mixed in with many lower-paying ones. And there's no way to tell, unless the slot has a sign indicating its payback percentage. A rarity in most casinos today, and prohibited in Atlantic City.

So ignore a sign with "up to" in it. In a carousel or bank of 20 slots, you'd be lucky to find one or two that pay back the high percentage advertised.

Look instead for a sign that says ALL SLOTS IN THIS AREA GUARANTEED TO RETURN... or ALL SLOTS IN THIS AREA CERTIFIED TO RETURN...plus a given percentage (97%, 98%). You won't find many. But when you do find one, bet max coin at every slot you try in that area.

*You get out of everything just what you put into it —
except in the case of slots.*

Casino Player's SLOT CHART

A slot is programmed to return to its players a percentage of all the coins put into it. The percentages below represent the average percent payback of the slot denominations shown. The figures will change periodically, but not by very much. For a full description of percentage payback, see **1. Percentage Payback** on page 6.

ATLANTIC CITY	25¢		50¢		$1		$5	
October, 2000	#SLOTS	WIN%	#SLOTS	WIN%	#SLOTS	WIN%	#SLOTS	WIN%
ATLANTIC CITY HILTON	1,147	91.7	195	90.8	312	92.5	60	95.4
BALLY'S PARK PLACE	2,253	91.4	420	92.2	533	92.4	94	94.1
CAESARS	1,931	90.8	447	91.6	600	93.3	102	93.6
CLARIDGE	1,275	91.4	127	90.2	225	92.1	36	94.0
HARRAH'S AC	1,704	91.9	222	92.7	586	92.6	104	95.6
RESORTS	1,512	91.1	215	91.7	322	93.0	53	97.5
SANDS	1,116	91.6	195	91.5	324	93.0	66	95.5
SHOWBOAT	2,248	90.8	212	89.0	462	90.6	69	95.1
TROPICANA	2,031	90.6	427	91.1	712	91.7	121	94.6
TRUMP MARINA	1,465	91.5	204	91.7	430	92.9	85	93.8
TRUMP PLAZA	1,679	91.5	246	92.4	376	90.8	70	94.2
TRUMP TAJ MAHAL	2,969	90.2	310	90.2	604	92.1	102	96.6

COLORADO	5¢		25¢		$1		$5	
September, 2000	#SLOTS	WIN%	#SLOTS	WIN%	#SLOTS	WIN%	#SLOTS	WIN%
BLACK HAWK	2,666	93.1	3,456	94.4	1,843	95.3	202	96.0
CENTRAL CITY	686	93.3	701	95.3	387	95.9	27	95.3
CRIPPLE CREEK	1,539	93.4	1,560	94.2	888	95.4	102	96.6

CONNECTICUT	25¢		50¢		$1		$5	
October, 2000	#SLOTS	WIN%	#SLOTS	WIN%	#SLOTS	WIN%	#SLOTS	WIN%
FOXWOODS	3,401	91.0	763	91.0	1,380	91.8	216	94.5
MOHEGAN SUN	1,476	91.1	365	91.1	1,004	92.1	149	93.9

NEVADA	5¢		25¢		$1		$5	
September, 2000	#SLOTS	WIN%	#SLOTS	WIN%	#SLOTS	WIN%	#SLOTS	WIN%
BALANCE OF COUNTY	6,821	94.0	9,439	96.3	2,798	96.7	227	97.2
BOULDER STRIP	7,710	93.5	6,460	96.7	1,713	97.2	114	97.9
DOWNTOWN-LV	5,977	92.3	8,416	95.1	2,571	95.6	222	96.8
LAKE TAHOE	1,362	92.3	3,001	93.7	1,453	95.7	212	97.0
LAS VEGAS STRIP	13,006	91.3	28,949	92.9	13,271	95.0	1,811	95.9
LAUGHLIN	3,207	91.1	5,724	94.6	2,031	96.1	210	96.2
MESQUITE	1,401	93.2	1,171	95.5	441	95.6	36	98.0
NORTH LAS VEGAS	3,190	94.6	2,984	97.2	598	97.9	N/A	N/A
RENO	6,505	93.4	7,948	94.2	4,283	96.1	517	96.3

ILLINOIS	5¢		25¢		$1		$5	
September, 2000	#SLOTS	WIN%	#SLOTS	WIN%	#SLOTS	WIN%	#SLOTS	WIN%
ALTON BELLE II	201	92.1	368	94.1	239	95.7	22	96.1
PAR-A-DICE	186	92.0	531	93.3	239	93.8	21	96.3
JUMER'S CASINO	176	92.7	314	93.9	89	95.2	11	95.0
JOLIET EMPRESS	171	88.8	414	93.0	389	94.0	51	95.8
METROPOLIS PLAYERS	234	91.3	384	92.3	348	94.4	45	95.6
HARRAH'S JOLIET	163	90.0	390	92.4	458	94.3	39	95.1
HOLLYWOOD	65	89.9	348	92.7	460	95.1	72	95.9
CASINO QUEEN	140	92.3	470	94.3	380	95.4	37	97.0
GRAND VICTORIA	—	—	354	92.7	447	95.2	92	96.2

IOWA	5¢		25¢		$1		$5	
October, 2000	#SLOTS	WIN%	#SLOTS	WIN%	#SLOTS	WIN%	#SLOTS	WIN%
ISLE OF CAPRI DAVENPORT	276	92.4	455	93.5	209	94.7	20	96.9
ISLE OF CAPRI BETTENDORF	328	92.9	443	93.0	273	95.0	37	96.0
AMERISTAR	668	92.0	419	93.6	306	95.5	50	96.1
HARVEYS	412	91.8	452	93.7	281	95.3	36	94.0
ISLE OF CAPRI MARQUETTE	181	91.9	375	93.0	180	95.3	13	96.0
DIAMOND JO	177	92.1	266	93.0	177	95.0	15	95.5
MISSISSIPPI BELLE II	96	91.6	298	93.0	103	93.9	6	96.1
CATFISH BEND	99	91.1	283	91.9	149	93.3	7	95.4
BELLE OF SIOUX CITY	192	92.5	154	93.0	76	95.2	5	97.2
LAKESIDE	191	91.8	409	94.2	215	94.2	28	95.4
PRAIRIE MEADOWS	261	91.8	583	93.3	369	95.0	46	96.9
BLUFFS RUN	303	92.5	705	93.8	431	95.8	38	96.6
DUBUQUE	178	91.7	248	92.9	164	94.9	10	95.1

LOUISIANA	5¢		25¢		$1		$5	
September, 2000	#SLOTS	WIN%	#SLOTS	WIN%	#SLOTS	WIN%	#SLOTS	WIN%
BATON ROUGE	547	91.8	557	93.3	442	94.8	59	96.1
LAKE CHARLES	551	91.4	1,502	91.2	973	93.1	126	94.6
NEW ORLEANS	2,080	92.0	2,809	92.7	1,189	94.9	156	96.2
SHREVEPORT/BOSSIER	545	91.1	1,857	92.1	1,708	94.3	260	95.3

MISSISSIPPI	5¢		25¢		$1		$5	
September, 2000	#SLOTS	WIN%	#SLOTS	WIN%	#SLOTS	WIN%	#SLOTS	WIN%
COASTAL REGION	4,983	92.1	6,370	93.1	3,381	95.6	467	96.1
NORTH RIVER REGION	2,940	91.1	6,328	92.2	4,332	95.2	616	96.0
SOUTH RIVER REGION	2,668	91.7	1,592	93.1	1,291	95.1	175	94.7

INDIANA	25¢		50¢		$1		$5	
September, 2000	#SLOTS	WIN%	#SLOTS	WIN%	#SLOTS	WIN%	#SLOTS	WIN%
ARGOSY LAWRENCEBURG	1,007	92.6	192	94.3	489	94.9	66	96.1
AZTAR EVANSVILLE	519	90.9	93	90.0	480	92.2	64	95.4
BLUE CHIP CASINO	691	91.7	82	92.7	421	94.3	53	94.8
CAESARS	1,447	92.1	231	92.4	554	94.5	84	94.5

	25¢		50¢		$1		$5	
	#SLOTS	WIN%	#SLOTS	WIN%	#SLOTS	WIN%	#SLOTS	WIN%
EMPRESS HAMMOND	600	91.7	150	92.2	609	94.4	71	94.8
GRAND VICTORIA	677	91.5	60	91.8	462	93.5	54	95.8
HARRAH'S	692	91.6	78	91.0	723	94.3	60	94.8
MAJESTIC STAR	618	92.0	51	92.6	480	94.7	62	97.5
TRUMP CASINO	536	92.2	69	92.5	448	94.3	28	95.1

MISSOURI	**25¢**		**50¢**		**$1**		**$5**	
September, 2000	#SLOTS	WIN%	#SLOTS	WIN%	#SLOTS	WIN%	#SLOTS	WIN%
ARGOSY RIVERSIDE	694	94.2	55	94.8	225	96.4	18	97.1
AZTAR CARUTHERSVILLE	463	90.3	—	—	189	90.5	5	95.5
HARRAH'S NORTH KC	1,292	93.1	70	93.3	451	95.4	47	96.0
HARRAH'S ST. LOUIS	2,061	93.4	129	93.9	613	95.5	61	96.5
ISLE OF CAPRI	313	94.4	16	93.1	146	95.8	16	97.7
KANSAS CITY STATION	1,999	93.2	120	94.0	550	95.6	56	97.0
PRESIDENT (ADMIRAL)	717	93.3	53	93.9	257	95.1	18	94.3
ST. CHARLES STATION	1,064	93.4	100	94.9	325	95.0	28	97.4
ST. JO FRONTIER	300	93.3	—	—	92	94.4	2	94.3

NOTE: If your state's casinos don't appear in this chart, it's because the state's gaming regulatory agencies don't release the information. Also, Native American casinos are not required to make their payback percentages public.

Reprinted with permission of *Casino Player* magazine.

3. Hit Frequency. Slots are programmed to pay out small amounts frequently to keep the player interested. It's called the hit frequency. It's the casino's way of heeding the wise old shepherd's saying, "You can shear a sheep many times, but you can only skin it once."

Most single payline slots have a hit frequency of 1 in 6 or 7 spins. The multicoin, multiline slots have a higher hit frequency (1 in 3 or 4 spins) *but only when all paylines are lit.*

To determine the hit frequency of a machine you're playing, simply count the number of spins between hits. Here are the average hit frequencies of some of today's slots:

Bingo	(Every 2-3 spins)	Reel 'em In	(Every 3-4 spins)
Double Diamond	(Every 6-7 spins)	Roarin' 20s	(Every 2-3 spins)
Empire	(Every 3 spins)	Smokin' Sevens	(Every 6-7 spins)
Filthy Rich	(Every 3-4 spins)	Sphinx	(Every 3-4 spins)
Jackpot Party	(Every 2-3 spins)	Top Cat	(Every 6 spins)
Jungle King	(Every 3 spins)	Treasure Tunnel	(Every 7-8 spins)
K.G. Bird	(Every 2-3 spins)	Wild Cougar	(Every 7-8 spins)
Polly & Roger	(Every 3 spins)	Wining Streak	(Every 6 spins)

Source: *Strictly Slots* magazine

4. *"Hey, he got my jackpot!"* If you see someone hit a big jackpot on the very first spin of the slot you just left, don't feel bad. It was just the luck of timing. You wouldn't have hit that jackpot even if you had stayed and made that next pull. The lucky player just happened to catch the jackpot symbol combination that existed at that split millisecond in the computer program.

The odds against your having hit the same winning symbol combination the exact, precise moment the lucky player did are astronomical! Even a few seconds makes a big difference. For example, in the time it takes for you to bend over and pick up a coin that fell to the floor, the computer will have played out hundreds of win-loss symbol combinations.

So rest easy. No one can steal your jackpot. Again, it's all a matter of luck and computer timing. *The number or sequence of handle pulls or hits of the "spin" button has nothing to do with it!*

5. *"It's due." "It's bound to hit."* Many players believe that if a particular slot has received a lot of play without paying off, it's due for a payoff and is a good slot to play. But a slot is never due, overdue, or bound to hit, no matter how much time and money you or another player may have put into it. The slot's computer has no timer or counter that triggers a payout based solely on

S	M	T	W	T	F	S
1	2	3	4	5	6	7
8	9	10	11	12	13	14
15	16	17	18	19	20	21
22	23	24	25	26	27	28
29	30					

the amount of time or money played. *All payouts are spread out over time and completely at random!*

Runs up to 20 spins without a hit are not uncommon. And a slot can go for days, weeks, or even months without paying out the top jackpot. Then it can pay out two or more top jackpots in one day. Pure mathematical randomness.

Many losing players desperate to win cling to the idea of a slot being due, overdue, or bound to hit. This is a common belief in gambling. It's called the gambler's fallacy. But in a game of chance like slots, nothing is ever due or overdue.

Each spin of the reels is completely independent of every other spin —meaning that no matter how many times you pull the handle or press the button, each spin has the same probability of winning (or losing). So whatever happened on the last dozen or so spins of the reels will have absolutely nothing to do with what's going to happen when you make the next spin.

> *A slot is never "due", "overdue", or "bound to hit" no matter how much time or money you or another player may have put into it!*

The Overdue Slot

Two slot machines got married in one of those quickie Las Vegas wedding chapels. Three months later, Mrs. Slot snuggled up to her mate and whispered, "Honey, I think I'm overdue."

*A **man was playing** a slot machine at 3:00 a.m. in a quiet corner of a casino. Suddenly he felt a chill and looked around. He was startled to see a ghost in a red dress pointing to a slot and saying, "Play that machine over there."*
The man jumped up and ran to the security desk, telling the security guard what he saw.
"Was the ghost wearing a red dress?" asked the guard.
"Yes!" exclaimed the frightened player.
"Oh, don't pay any attention to her," said the guard. "She didn't have any luck picking slots when she was alive."

*A **feeble old man** in his nineties suffered a stroke after hitting a 10-million-dollar pot on a Megabucks slot. But with the loving care of his family and his kind and devoted nurse, he never recovered.*

*A **teacher giving a class** on modern inventions asks a gambler's son, "Billy, can you name anything of importance that didn't exist ten years ago?"*
Gambler's son: "Video slots."

2
WINNING STREAKS AND LOSING STREAKS

Slot machines are programmed to pay out their percentages stochastically. Which is the technical way of saying randomly. And it's this randomness that causes all kinds of streaks to occur. Few good. Most bad.

Winning streaks are rare and don't last long. So it's important to recognize at what point a winning streak ends and a losing one begins. The only problem is it's hard to tell when one streak ends and another begins. So what do you do? It's your call. There are no hard and fast rules. But the following guidelines should help you.

 Winning Streak. Wow! You can't believe it! You're hitting on every third or fourth spin. Stay at this slot as long as you keep winning. There's no limit to playing while you're winning. And this is one of the times to bet max coin.

> *Old Gambler's Saying*
> *"When your luck begins to run out, it keeps on running."*

 Losing Streak. You're on a winning streak. Then, as you keep playing, you suddenly realize that nothing is happening. No more wins of any kind! A clear sign that a losing streak has begun.

Common sense tells you to quit, but you keep playing anyway. Quitting a slot you've been winning at isn't easy. You're convinced that if you just keep playing long enough, you're sure to start winning again.

But the more you lose, the more you become committed to that slot — desperately hoping that your luck will turn around. But a cold slot is like a dead love affair. When it's over, it's over!

13

Other signs that your luck has made a U-turn are the growing feelings of anger and frustration with each losing spin. Plus the sinking feeling in your stomach that you're putting it all back in.

A good way to force yourself to quit during a losing streak is to say to yourself, "Hey, this slot's cold!" Then set a limit to the number of losing spins in a row you're going to make (3, 4, ? spins). Call it a **losing-spin limit.**

If you reach this losing-spin limit, call it quits. No saying to yourself, "Just one more spin" over and over and over again. Be prepared to walk away from a cold slot at any time. Don't wait until icicles start forming on it!

Should you win again before hitting your losing-spin limit, keep playing. But set a new losing-spin limit. Setting a losing-spin limit after each win keeps you playing during a hot streak and will warn you when a cold streak has begun.

"Casino Quotes"

All slots are alike. But they look different so you can tell them apart.

Chasing after a megajackpot is a difficult pursuit.

Casinos prove the old saying that when you get something for nothing you're paying a high price for it.

Poker is a game in which a good deal depends on a good deal.

A lot of the people you see in a casino get their only exercise by pushing their luck.

The only certainty about gambling is its uncertainty.

My wife is an obsessive slot player. If heaven doesn't have slot machines, she ain't going.

In a casino, an ounce of common sense is worth a ton of luck.

Man vs. Machine

A player doesn't mind losing a few dollars at a machine. He can walk away without giving it too much thought. At this point, he has no real commitment to the game.

But say he loses $50 or more, now he must face the fact that if he quits without a win, all his investment has been lost. So he wages a frantic all-out battle with the machine in the dim hope of recouping some of his losses.

And the more he loses, the more hold the soulless machine has over him. Caution, coin, and common sense are swept aside. Winning becomes an obsession. And in the end the machine usually prevails.

Still the hapless player continues the losing battle, giving up only when he's wiped out. Then he slinks away sadder but usually no wiser. The inevitable fate of the the player who stays too long at a cold slot.

Remember: A slot machine is programmed to take your money. So it's only logical to program yourself to stop playing when it starts taking too much. And that's where a losing-spin limit comes in. It's a red alert telling you when to let go. And the sooner you let go, the easier it is to walk away.

—Old Gambler's Saying—
A good gambler knows when to quit winners.
A better gambler knows when to quit losers.

The Bridge to Hawaii

A man was walking along a California beach and came across an old lamp lying in the sand. He picked it up, rubbed it, and out popped an old, wizened genie. In an exasperated tone, the genie said, "Hey, this is the fourth time this month I've been picked up. And I'm getting a little tired of granting three wishes. So, buddy, you're going to get only one wish. Now, what is it?"

The man thought a while, then said, "I've always wanted to go to Hawaii, but I'm afraid to fly and I get seasick. Could you build me a bridge to Hawaii?"

The genie laughed and said, "Why, that's impossible! How could the bridge supports reach to the bottom of the ocean? Think how much concrete, how much steel. No, I can't do that. Think of another wish."

Again, the man thought, then said, "I go to Las Vegas two or three times a year to play the slots. And I lose every time. I've read books on the game, talked to professional slot players, subscribed to all kinds of gaming magazines. But no matter what I've read or studied I keep losing every time. So if there's a secret way to beat the slots, tell me. I command you."

The genie replied, "Do you want that bridge with two lanes or four?"

During a roulette session a fly happened to land on 34 red. Taking this as a good luck omen, a player put all he had on this number. The wheel spun, and the ball landed on 17 red. "Too bad," a fellow player said. "It must have been a house fly."

A gambler's son is being quizzed by a history teacher.
Teacher: "What is a monarchy?"
Son: "A people governed by a king."
Teacher: "Right. And who would reign if the king died?"
Son: "The queen."
Teacher: "And if the queen should die?"
Son: "The jack."

3

TYPE OF SLOT TO PLAY

Whatever denomination slot you choose to play, stick to the 2-coin, 3-reel, single-payline, nonprogressive slot with the lowest top jackpot (1000-5000 coins).

And before playing those dazzling 3-D video, touchscreen, or player-interactive slots, be sure to read the playing instructions carefully. Most players just glance at a slot's instructions. They really don't read to understand. They go to a casino to have fun, not to read instructions.

But that's just what you should do if you decide to play an unfamiliar slot. Read the instructions. If you have trouble understanding, watch other people playing the same model slot for a while. And don't be afraid to ask them questions. They'll usually be glad to help.

As a last resort, summon the change person. If they can't help you, they'll summon someone who can.

Bottom line: Don't be seduced into putting money into a slot, no matter how enticing, until you know how it works.

1. The 3-Payline Slot. You have more chances of winning on this type of slot, but the payouts tend to be small. And the top prize is usually paid only if you line up the winning symbols on the bottom (or third) line — which means that you must always bet three coins for a 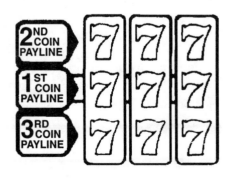 shot at the jackpot. Avoid this kind of slot. Your gambling dollar will be better spent on the two-coin maximum, three-reel, single-payline slot.

If you like playing three-payline slots but don't like to bet max coin, try this: Bet just one coin. If you win, bet two coins. If you win again, bet three coins. If the slot turns cold, drop down to one-coin bets, or walk away.

2. Finding the Right Slots to Play.

Casinos want players to see other players winning. So they often put their loosest slots in certain heavy-traffic areas and locations visible from many directions on the casino floor — such as slot squares, crosswalks, and elevated carousels ...with room for small crowds to gather and cheer winners on.

Casinos know it's good advertising for visitors to hear the clatter of coins dropping into a tray and see winners jumping up and down and shrieking with joy. A scene that motivates visitors to start playing and current players to play harder. So the three magic words to remember are: *visibility, visibility, visibility.*

Each casino has its own slot-placement philosophy. So the slot floor layout will vary from casino to casino. And it's a closely guarded secret. The slot floor layout is decided by the casino's slot manager, who constantly looks at what machines are getting heavy play and what locations are doing best. So player psychology, game popularity, and traffic patterns are major factors in his slot-placement decisions.

Here's a fun exercise for you. Pretend you're the slot manager of the casino you're visiting. Using high visibility and heavy traffic patterns as slot-placement criteria, where would you put your loosest slots?

The loosest slots are generally visible from many directions and vantage points on the casino floor.

3. Most Likely Places to Find Loose Slots. The following suggestions will help you find the right spots and slots to play. But remember, they're just that: suggestions. You'll have to conduct your own Columbo-type search and investigation.

Treat every slot you approach as a suspect. Study the clues it gives off. They'll tell you whether it's worth playing. Also, snoop around. Grill current players and slot floor personnel. The clues are out there. Look for them!

Here are some helpful clues to the loosest slots:

* Near a casino bar, lounge, cashier's cage, or change booth. *(All highly visible areas!)*

* In an area with sign reading ALL SLOTS CERTIFIED TO RETURN or ALL SLOTS GUARANTEED TO RETURN, plus a given percentage. The key word in the sign is ALL. Ignore a sign with the words UP TO or AVERAGE in it.

* Slots *just off* a busy aisle in row after row of slots.

* A bank of slots against a wall on an aisle with heavy traffic to your back.

* Heavy foot-traffic areas: busy walkways, crosswalks, and at the beginning and end of traffic patterns (moving walkways, top and bottom of stairways and escalators).

* On riverboats: at the entrance to the boarding dock.

4. Avoid These Slots and Spots:

* Near show lines, check-in lines, buffet lines. *(The "impulse" slots. Slots designed to catch the occasional coins of people who step out of line to try their luck while waiting.)*

* Near elevators and restrooms *(Unattractive areas).*

* In the middle of rows of slots facing each other. If you have no choice, try the slots *nearest* the aisle.

19

* Giant linked progressives like Megabucks, Nevada Nickels, Quartermania, Win-a-Car, and similar multireel linked slots. The odds on your state lottery are probably better.

* Airports, gas stations, cruise ships, and other nongaming areas, where people play just to pass the time. *(Very low percentage payback in these areas!)*

* Near keno, race and sports book, and gaming tables. *(Slot and people noises annoy and distract players in these areas, so casinos don't put their player-friendly slots near them.)*

* Big Berthas. These are those giant dollar slots with huge handles, usually located near casino entrances. They're mostly advertising gimmicks. But they're fun to watch *others* play.

* "Slot Joints." These are those small casinos with doors open to the sidewalk, blaring music, and some type of spin-the-wheel deal or a costumed character (clown, cowboy) handing out coupons for freebies inside. Once you're inside, they use tricks to keep you there. They're mostly tourist traps.

* Out-of-the-way corners and remote areas of the casino. *(Although casinos sprinkle loose slots throughout the casino, winners in low-traffic areas like these have little advertising value for the casino.)*

* A slot with 4, 5, 6 reels *(All multicoin, multiline video games).*

* A slot with 5 or more paylines — accepting up to 20 coins per line.

* A slot with mid-range jackpot of 10,000 to 50,000 coins.

* Crowded casino with few of your favorite slots to choose from, or where you have to stand in line to play.

* The virtual casino (on-line slot playing on the Internet). It could be habit forming!

5. Looking for Mr. Right Slot. Instead of drifting aimlessly from slot to slot looking for the golden needle in the slot haystack, let other slot players do some of the looking for you. Here's how:

(1) Carrying a small pad and pencil, stroll casually about the slot floor. Look for slots that are getting lots of action and paying out big. (Don't cover the entire casino. Just do one section at a time.)

Ask yourself: Are the slots in an area that meets the criteria of heavy traffic and high visibility? If so, sketch out their locations in the pad. Jotting down the serial numbers is also helpful. Come back later and give them a try. Helpful tip: The pad could also be used to record your wins and  losses for income tax purposes, as discussed in Section 13, THE IRS WINS TOO.

(2) Spend some time just observing other players. That is, sit at a slot near a carousel or bank of slots where you can watch the comings and goings of players.

Note which slots pay out regularly. Especially watch for a player who's getting small but consistent wins and putting it all back in.

While observing, pretend you're playing the slot you're sitting at. Try not to stare. People get nervous when they know they're being watched.

How long do you watch? That's up to you. Just take your time. When finished, you might even check your findings with the resident change person, carousel attendant, or slot attendant. See how close your findings agree. It's a good presession or break activity. And by narrowing down the universe of slots to choose from, you'll get a better selection of slots to play.

Being a slot voyeur isn't much fun, but it costs nothing. And it could turn out to be one of the best investments you can make in a casino.

Some slot pros say that observing players at certain machines is part of their strategy.

6. Beware of These Slots

* Buy-A-Pay. A straight slot will reward all hits, giving a higher percentage payback when max coins are played. With a buy-a-pay, however, each coin buys you a different set of winning symbol combinations. For example, in a 3-coin version of the slot:

* 1 coin pays only on a winning combination involving only one type of symbol - such as cherries

* 2 coins pay on winning symbol combinations involving two kinds of symbols - such as cherries and bars

* 3 coins pay off on the top jackpot and all other winning symbol combinations shown on the pay table.

If you hit a 7-7-7 on a buy-a-pay with just one or two coins in, you get nothing.

You can recognize a buy-a-pay by looking at the payout table. In a three-coin version, it'll show the winning symbol combination when one coin is played, a second group when two coins are played, and a third group when max coins are played. That's why it's important to read the payout table of every slot you play.

Like a progressive, the buy-a-pay is a machine where you must always bet max coin. And with a hit frequency of 1 in 7-8, it's best to avoid.

* Any Progressive Slot *(Quartermania, Cool Millions, etc.).* Playing progressive slots with the top jackpot in mind is a very unrealistic goal. To win big, you must always bet max coin against ridiculously high house odds (as low as 85% payback).

They also have more reels or more symbols per reel, making it harder to line up the winning symbols. That's why it's smarter to stay with the simple 2-coin, 3-reel, single-payline, nonprogressive slot at whatever denomination you choose to play. You'll win small jackpots more often. And for most people, that's the fun way to play.

But if playing progressives is what you like, stick to the 2-coin, 3-reel, single-payline, stand-alone, in-house progressive. Chances of hitting are more realistic. And bet max coin up to the amount you can afford to lose.

It's true that some wannabe millionaire will eventually hit one of the blockbuster jackpots. But anchoring yourself to just one of the megaprogressives and fixating on the top prize is like buying roundtrip tickets on the Titanic. You can kiss your money bon voyage.

Here's a better idea from the sultan of slots, Frank Scoblete, for playing superslots like Megabucks, Cool Millions, Dollars Deluxe, etc.:

> *"No matter how many there are in the casino, play them all! And always bet max coin for a total of three spins per slot. That's three max-coin spins for Megabucks, three max-coin spins for Dollars Deluxe, etc.*
>
> *"Even if you win 20 or more coins per machine, move on. That's because these monsters don't return enough of the smaller hits to make it worthwhile to get a run going."*

Frank has a good idea here. In fact, the next time you hear or read of a player who has hit a big jackpot, see if they invested only

$10 to $40 and played only 5 to 20 minutes before hitting. A common occurrence, since most players who try their luck on the giants do so for only a few bucks to see what happens. They then move on to the slots where they know they have a better chance of winning.

In his book *Bad Bet*, former Wall Street Journal reporter Timothy L. O'Brien said this about megajackpot-type machines, "Megabucks jackpots keep getting larger until someone wins. And just as in a lottery, chances of winning stink."

Final tip. If you insist on playing Megabucks and the other millionaire makers, save them for the last day or part of your trip. The final adrenaline rush will add a touch of excitement to your casino experience.

 Avoid progressives — the Titanic of bankroll disasters. But if you insist, bet max coin up to the amount you can afford to lose.

How's The Wife?
A tourist spots a friend playing slots in an Atlantic City casino.
Tourist: "Hey, Bill. Nice seeing you. How's your luck?"
Player: "Rotten. Really rotten."
Tourist: "Too bad. And how's your wife?"
Player: "About the same."

A sign in a casino *pool area warned: DON'T GO INTO THE WATER AFTER A BIG MEAL. Beneath the warning someone wrote, "You'll never find one there."*

Dining in the Monte Carlo Casino *restaurant on the French Riviera, an American tourist was sitting at a table next to a party of Americans who were having trouble with the French menu. He got up and went over to the leader of the group.*
"Excuse me. I'm an American too. And I see you're having trouble ordering a dinner. I'll be glad to help you if I can."
"No thanks," said the group leader sourly. "We don't need nor want your help." "Sorry," said the good Samaritan. "I thought maybe you did. I just heard you order a flight of steps."

4
SLOT MYTH AND REALITY

Slot players are among the most superstitious people in the world. They develop a blind belief in any notion they think will give them an edge. And nothing you can say will make them give it up, no matter how impractical or foolish you show it to be. Generally, most slot superstitions are harmless and won't help or hurt your playing. For example:

Myth **There are certain days of the week or time of the day or night that is better to play than any other.**

Reality When you play one of today's one-armed bandits, you're playing a computer in slot's clothing. And the computer doesn't know or care whether it's a weekend or weekday or what time of the day or night it is. So there is no "best" time to play slot machines.

Myth **A player sits at a slot you just left and with the very first pull of the handle hits a jackpot. He stole your jackpot!**

Reality The slot's computer program generates a different win-loss symbol combination *every millisecond*, 24 hours a day, 7 days a week, whether the machine is being played or not. Even if you had stayed and made that next pull, the odds against your hitting the winning symbol combination the exact same millisecond the lucky player did are astronomical!

So no one stole your jackpot. It was just a matter of luck and computer timing.

Myth **If the coins in the tray feel warm, it means they've been in the slot a long time and it's ready to pay off.**

Reality The only part of this myth that's true is that the coins have been in the slot a long time, perhaps hours. And during this time, they were exposed to internal light bulbs and other heat sources. Conversely, if the coins feel cold, they were recently taken from a cool, air-conditioned counting room and placed in the slot or were circulated internally by heavy play.

Myth **If you see a player walk away from a slot they have played for a long time and got little or nothing back, it's been warmed up for you and it's a good one to play.**

Reality It doesn't matter how much time or money you or another player may have put into a slot. All payouts are spread out over time and completely at random. You might hit on the very first spin or go up to 20 spins without hitting anything. A close cousin of this myth is that empty coin wrappers around a slot are a sign that a player gave that slot heavy play without winning. But who's to say the player didn't walk away a winner?

Myth **Avoid playing a slot that is nearly empty of coins or one that has just been serviced by a slot technician.**

Reality This is one of the sillier myths. It makes no difference to the slot's computer whether the coin hopper is full or nearly empty of coins. And how is a player supposed to know? Also, a slot technician performing routine maintenance or repair has no effect on a slot's payout.

Myth **If you play a slot as fast as you can, you have a better chance of winning.**

Reality Playing a slot at warp speed has no effect on the computer's selection of win-loss symbol combinations. The faster you play, the faster you go through your bankroll and playing time.

Myth **Change persons and other slot floor personnel usually know what slots are "hot" and ready to pay off.**

Reality As mentioned elsewhere, slot floor personnel may know what slots have been paying out in their area, but there's no guarantee they'll continue to do so.

Besides, if they really knew where the "hot" slots were, wouldn't it make sense to tell a special friend or relative? And if a really big jackpot was involved, what's to stop them from quitting their job and playing the "hot" slots themselves?

Myth **Pulling the handle gives you more control than pressing the spin button.**

Reality It makes no difference how you start the reels spinning. Either way, you're just telling the computer to display on the screen the win-loss symbol combination it has chosen for you. But by pulling the handle, you slow down your game and lose calories too!

Myth **A slot's computer can tell the difference between max-coin play and short-coin play.**

Reality The slot's computer doesn't care how many coins you put in. The number of coins inserted has no effect on whether you win or lose. Just how much you win or lose.

Myth **Slots near casino entrances pay better.**

Reality Today's casinos don't need to lure passers-by to come in and play. It was done in the early days. But putting higher-paying slots near entrances is rarely done. Except on riverboats. Casino floor designers tend to place themed attractions, live musical groups, win-a-car displays, and the more popular machines up front to create an attractive gaming environment and the appearance of winning activity. They call it the "shill" area. They know that a pleasant gaming environment is the shortest path to the player's bankroll.

Myth **If you've been playing a slot that has paid off two or more times in a row, stop playing. The theory of probability says that it's going to turn cold.**

Reality The theory of probability is a mathematical prediction of what may be expected to happen. Not what must inevitably happen. A slot that came up with three 7s five minutes ago

27

is just as likely to come up three 7s in the next spin. Slot machines have no memory any more than dice do.

Myth   **Casinos make their slots tighter on weekends and holidays.**

Reality   Although it takes just a few minutes to change a computer chip to make a slot tighter, no casino would ever consider tightening up every single slot on the floor. Why bother? They already have a built-in mathematical edge on every bet made — guaranteeing them a sure, steady profit. Besides, the gaming authority in each state has strict rules about changing a slot's payout percentage on the casino floor. It's not all that easy. A lot of paperwork is involved.

Myth   **Always put your coins in with the head facing out.**

Reality   The slot's coin reader doesn't care which way you put the coins in.

Myth   **There are certain things you can do to a slot that will improve your odds.**

Reality   There is nothing a player can do to a slot externally that will increase their chances to win. Still, some players naively believe they can. Here are just a few of the silly things they do in an attempt to outwit the slot:

· Feed in coins fast or slow
· Heat coins with a cigarette lighter to expand the coin-payout mechanism, forcing coins out
· Jerk or jiggle the handle
· Hold the handle down until the reels stop
· Chill coins with ice cubes to "startle" the slot into paying out
· Pull the handle down fast or slow
· Sprinkle salt on the slot for luck
· Quickly alternate pulling the handle and hitting the spin button (pull-spin, spin-pull...or..pull-pull, spin-spin, etc.) to "confuse" the slot

- Pour soft drinks down the coin acceptor to trip the payout mechanism
- Anthropomorphize the slot by (1) *entreaty*: begging, pleading, cajoling, praying to, or by (2) *slot rage*: kicking punching, hitting, swearing at.

Warning: A player who attempts to interfere with the normal operation of a slot machine is subject to arrest for tampering with the slot.

Myth   **Slots on the aisle or at the end of a row pay better.**

Reality   Although slots in these locations are highly visible, they don't necessarily pay better than slots in other areas. They only seem to pay better because a lot of people believe this myth and play them more often.

Myth   **When you're at a really "hot" slot that's paying out like crazy, a slot attendant will come over, open it up, and do something to stop it from paying out again.**

Reality   There is no switch or button in a slot that can be pressed to prevent a slot from paying out or hitting a big jackpot.

Reality   When a slot attendant sees a machine that seems to be paying out more than average for that model, he may open it up, but just to see that the slot's computer program is functioning properly.

Myth   **If you stay at a slot long enough, it's bound to pay off.**

Reality   Maybe yes. Maybe no. If you pick a slot with a low 80% payback, chances are you'll run out of money before you hit a sizable pot. Slot payouts are 100% random. So no slot is ever "bound to pay off" no matter how much time or money you or another player may have put into it.

Myth   **Casinos pump oxygen into the gaming area to keep the players alert so they can gamble for longer periods of time without becoming tired.**

Reality   All upscale casinos have state-of-the-art air-purification systems to keep the casino indoor environment fresh and clean. The purified air helps players and employees feel better. It's also illegal for a casino to pump pure oxygen into its gaming areas.

Myth   **You have a better chance of winning with a slot club card inserted in the card reader.**

Reality   Use of the slot club card has no effect on whether you win or lose or the size and number of payouts. The inserted card merely identifies you and the amount of your play for reward or future marketing purposes.

Myth   **It's best not to use a slot club card, since the IRS can get hold of the casino's records and see how much you've won or lost.**

Reality   Casinos give information to the IRS only when you hit a slot machine jackpot of $1200 or more. The IRS is not interested in the small wins of routine play at the machines.

Myth   **Slot machines go through cycles.**

Reality   When people talk about cycles, they refer to the theoretical number of spins for all the possible symbol combinations to come up, based on the computer program involved.

But since every symbol combination in today's slots is randomly selected by a computer program, there are no cycles. Only hot streaks and cold streaks. Mostly cold.

Finally, there are the superstitious hopefuls who touch big winners in hopes that their luck will rub off on them. If you do this, be careful whom you touch — and where.

In case of an earthquake, go to a keno lounge.
Nothing is ever hit in one.

5

BANKROLL AND COMFORT ZONE

Your bankroll is the amount of money you to take to the casino to gamble with. If, for example, you take $600 and plan to gamble for three days, your playing bankroll is $200 per day.

When this $200 is gone, your gambling for the day is over! If you borrow against the remaining $400, you run the risk of losing everything in one day and having nothing left for the remaining two days.

And don't even think about asking the casino credit manager for a line of credit...or visiting those ubiquitous casino ATMs, debit card, and credit card cash-advance machines. Playing with plastic will come back to haunt you when the bank statements start coming in.

Comfort zone refers to how you feel while playing at a particular denomination slot. If you're at a slot and you sweat every pull of the handle, you're out of your comfort zone.

A good rule to follow is to play at the denomination slot where you feel the most comfortable and which gives you the longest possible playing time for your money.

And this means playing s-l-o-w-l-y! Don't spin the reels the moment they stop. What's the rush? Relax! By taking your time you extend your playing time and the life of your bankroll.

The race is not always to the swift. Slow and steady is bound to win.

Here are some ways to slow yourself down:

(1) Stop hitting the spin button. Pull the handle for a while.

(2) Play with coins instead of credits.

(3) Pause between reel spins.

(4) Take frequent breaks.

(5) If sitting, get up occasionally. Stretch.

(6) Bet 1 coin.

(7) Stop. Look around. Watch other players nearby.

(8) Cash out accumulated credits. Feed coins in by hand.

(9) If playing with credits, hit PLAY ONE CREDIT button slowly three times, rather than hit PLAY MAX CREDIT button.

The following table shows the suggested slot level to play for your particular daily bankroll:

Comfort Zone Table

Daily Bankroll	Recommended Slot Levels
Up to $50	5¢
$50 to $100	5¢, 25¢
$100 to $200	25¢, 50¢, $1
$200 to $1000	50¢, $1, $5, $25

Play slow!
Make your bankroll and playing time last longer!

6
BET 1 COIN? 2 COINS? MAX COINS?

If there were a Surgeon General of slots, he or she would probably issue the following:

> **SURGEON GENERAL'S WARNING: Betting the maximum number of coins at all times is hazardous to your wealth.**

1. "Expert" Advice. Most slot "experts" will advise you to bet max coin at whatever denomination slot you choose to play. Sounds like good advice. But unless you're fabulously rich, incredibly optimistic, or enjoy giving your money to the casino...don't! It's an engraved invitation to the Broke-R-Us Club.

There are certain times to bet max coin. And you'll learn later on what they are. But for now, know that slots are programmed to take your money. And most of the time you're going to lose.

So ignore any "expert" or casino know-it-all who warns against betting less than max coin with the lame threat implied in "What if...?" They always stress the remote possibility of winning — dismissing or ignoring the greater reality of losing. In short, they shout WIN! But whisper *loooose*.

There's no "right" or "wrong" way to bet at a slot machine, no matter how loudly the "experts" protest there is. So tune out the bet-max mantra of the "experts" and other champions of max-coin play. Remember. It's not *their* money you're playing with!

Philosophies aside, how you bet depends on your mood, the size of your bankroll, and your personal playing style. Bottom line: Always play at a denomination slot that is appropriate for your bankroll and expectations.

2. Starting Out. If, like most people, you go to a casino to get away, have a few hours of fun, and maybe win a few bucks now and then, it doesn't really matter how you bet: maximum, minimum, or a combination of both. The true secret of slot playing is to make your bankroll and playing time last as long as possible. And this means keeping your losses down.

NOTE: The suggested playing strategy below is geared to the standard 2-coin, 3-reel, single-payline, nonprogressive slot. Sticking to 2-coin slots will save you money. And they often pay as well, and sometimes better, than 3-coin slots.

When starting out, ignore a PLAY MAX COIN sign on a slot. It's a psychological trap the casinos set with "what if?" as the bait. A few coins will tell you whether you're at a player-friendly slot or a coin-guzzling dud. And to keep from squandering your money on duds, start by betting just **one** coin for 3, 4, ? spins. Call it a **test-spin limit**.

If you lose 3, 4, ? times in a row, stop! Move on to the next slot. If you get a coin or two back (blank, cherries), play them off. Also **one** coin at a time.

If you start getting small but consistent wins, or the slot pays out like crazy, bet **2 coins**. And stay with it as long as it keeps paying. You may have found a high-percentage payback ("loose") slot. When it stops paying, set a losing-spin limit and move on. Setting losing-spin limits keeps you playing during a hot streak and warns you when a cold streak has begun.

There's an old Vegas saying, "To win big, you gotta bet big." But to bet big, you gotta have a big bankroll. And in a game of chance like slots where you're more likely to lose, small bets make more sense. They keep your losses down. Then when it comes time to bet max coin (discussed later), the Hamiltons ($10), Jacksons ($20) and Franklins ($100) will be there for you.

And should some nosy casino busybody ask why you're not betting max coin, just say that you're trying to build up a pot. Ignore the "What planet are you from?" stare.

It may be heartbreaking to miss out on the top prize by betting just one coin. But no big deal. Don't agonize over what you could have won. Focus on what you did win! *And how lucky you were to have won something at all!*

A player in Harrah's Las Vegas won $200 on a quarter slot with just one coin in. She confessed that had she bet max coin at every slot, she never would have gotten to the winning slot. So she had no trouble tuning out the good-natured jeers of her slot neighbors for winning a measly $200. *Moral:* Don't cry over a spilled jackpot.

3. Max-Coin Play. If you can afford to bet max coin at all times — and a *Casino Player* magazine poll revealed that 72% of the respondents do — then go ahead. Just be sure to keep in mind the idea of a test-spin limit and losing-spin limit at every slot you play.

4. Less Than Max-Coin Play. If you don't like or can't afford to bet max coin all the time, you can add variety and suspense to your playing by betting as follows:

2-coin slot	Use a 1-2 coin pattern (1 coin, 1 spin; 2 coins, 1 spin). This gives you a 50-50 chance at the top prize if you hit.
3-coin slot	Use a 1-2-3 coin pattern (1 coin, 1 spin; 2 coins, 1 spin; 3 coins, 1 spin). Or you can create any coin pattern you wish: 1-2-1-2, 2-2-2, 2-1-3, etc.
25-, 45-, 50-, 90-, 100-, 225-coin slots	The coinivores. OK to try for the fun or novelty. But only for a short time and a small amount.

Final betting tip: It's better to play one coin at the next higher denomination slot than max coin at the next lower one. For example, you get better odds playing 1 coin in a dollar slot than 4 to 5 coins in a quarter slot. See *Casino Player's* Slot Chart on page 8 for the difference in percentage payback.

Old Gambler's Saying
"Want to see time fly in a casino?
Bet max coin and play with credits."

5. Two-Coin Slots vs. Three-Coin Slots. Did you know that two-coin slots often pay out just as well as...and sometimes better than...three coin slots? Below are some payout table figures taken from a comparative study of dollar slot machines in Harrah's and the Flamingo Hilton, Las Vegas:*

Two-Coin Dollar Slots		Three-Coin Dollar Slots	
Haywire	$800-$1000	Haywire	$500-$1600-$2500
Double Diamond	$1000-$5000	Double Diamond	$800-$1600-$2500
Black & White	$2000-$5000	Triple Diamond	$1000-$2000-$4000
Red, White & Blue	$2000-$5000	Red, White & Blue	$2000-$4000-$10000
Wild Rose	$2500-$5000	Treasure Tunnel	$1000-$2000-$3000
Wild Cherry	$2500-$5000	Wild Cherry	$1000-$2500-$10000

October 2000

As you can see, you can't go wrong sticking with the two-coin slots. They offer decent jackpots, and your bankroll and playing time will last longer.

Follow this same two-coin betting strategy with all the other denomination slots you play. Why pay more to play?

================== Cheerful Advice ==================

Slot host to heavy loser: "Cheer up, Dame Fortune will come knocking at your door one of these days." "Well," said the loser, "she'll really have to knock. Her daughter, Miss Fortune, broke the bell."

A seventh-grade teacher asks a pupil, "Billy, what is an effigy?"
Pupil: "I don't know."
Teacher: "An effigy is a dummy. Now, Billy, can you use the word in a sentence?"
Pupil (thinks): "Oh! My father is a blackjack dealer in a casino, and every night at dinner he tells us about all the effigies that played at his table."

7
WELCOME TO THE CLUB!

It's a good idea to join the slot club (or player's club) of every major casino you play in — no matter how little or how often you play there. It's free. And when you sign up you become an instant VIP. But not every casino has one. You'll have to ask an employee of the casino whether it does.

If it does, you'll receive a plastic card (similar to the illustration) which you insert into the card reader of each slot you play. The points you get for playing are then tabulated in

(courtesy of Stardust, Las Vegas)

a computer, making you eligible for such "comps" as cash-back awards, free or discounted rooms, meals, show tickets, shark repellent, and other freemiums. You'll also receive periodic mailings from the casino with invitations to special events and deals not available to the general public.

"Comp" is short for complimentary. It's the casino's way of thanking you for your patronage and promoting customer loyalty. Just as airlines use frequent flyer miles to promote loyalty to a particular airline.

When you sign up at a slot club booth, ask how many cards you can get. Some card clubs issue only one, some two, some as many as you want. Policy varies. If you have a spouse, get one for him/her so you can accumulate points on one account.

The reason for multiple cards is that if you're with a spouse or friends who are not club members, ask them if they wouldn't mind using your card when they play.

If you forget to bring your card or leave it in a machine, go to the slot club booth. They'll gladly replace it for you — as a rule.

Most slot clubs don't automatically reward their loyal customers. Just the askers. So whatever casino slot club you're a member of, ask a slot host or at the slot club booth what comps you're entitled to. Or you can call from the privacy of your room, if a guest of the hotel. But ask!

Each casino has a distinctive name for its slot club: Total Gold (Harrah's), Emperors Club (Caesars Palace). In the Foxwoods Indian casino in CT, it's called the Wampum Club.

When making room reservations through a travel agent, mention that you're a member of the casino's slot club. If you phone the hotel directly, tell the reservation desk clerk that you're a member of the casino's slot club. And have your membership card handy. You'll be asked for your membership number to see whether you're entitled to a discounted room rate (the casino rate).

A few hotels automatically enroll their hotel guests in their slot club when they check in. All others can sign up at the slot club booth.

You'll find that some slot clubs are good — others so-so. But join as many slot clubs as you can. You'll be glad you did!

CAUTION: Don't get psyched into betting more or playing longer just to earn points for comps. You could end up spending more than they're worth. Think of comps as a bonus. Don't make them your goal. Losing $300 to get a $3.00 sandwich and a pickle is no bargain.

You really can't call them casinos.
They're more like a Bermuda Triangle for money.

8
SLOT-POURRI

A collection of slot wit and wisdom that will amuse and inform.

Forget what your mother told you about talking to strangers. Don't be afraid to ask current players how they're doing and about slots nearby. Many will be glad to share their experiences with you, pointing out which slots to try and which to avoid. And you might just luck out and bump into a "local"or "regular" willing to give you some helpful tips.

Have you noticed the increased use of small, round slot carousels — with four or so machines? The casino has two good reasons for installing them. First, it eliminates the need for a carousel attendant. Second, casinos know that people don't like sitting close to each other. The round configuration gives them more elbow room.

The timeless question: Can slot machines be beaten? "Of course," says gaming guru Frank Scoblete. "If you buy the right hammer and plant one or two whacks firmly on the belly glass, you should be able to get right to the money. A good drill would help as well. This is a great strategy for people who can't wait to go to jail."

Seriously, it's not possible to beat the slots in the long run. But you can come out ahead in any given session — the short run. Just follow the simple advice in this book on how to bet and set test-spin and losing-spin limits. If you do, you'll go a long way toward having more winning sessions.

♠♠♠♠

Does it really help to ask a change person, carousel attendant, or cocktail server for advice on what slots to play? Well, it's like chicken soup for a cold. It may not help. But it sure won't hurt.

Most of the above will gladly point out what slots they've seen hitting and those constantly being filled with coins. So they do have a general idea of where the better paying slots in their section are. But you must remember that even though a specific machine has been paying off in the last hour or so, there's no guarantee that it will continue to do so. Again, all payouts are completely random. You might hit it big. You might hit nothing.

Just don't tip up front for any advice proffered. Some players do for luck. But the real time to tip is *after* a win — and if you want to. Tipping is a bonus given for extra service. Not an obligation.

How much do you tip someone for steering you to a slot you've won at? It depends on how much you've won and how friendly and helpful that someone was to you. Here are some figures you can use as a tipping guideline:

Win	Suggested Tip
$100	$5
$500	$10
$1000	$20 ($40 is a very good tip)

Tipping a slot attendant or other casino employee who merely hand-pays a win is optional. Those who don't tip point out that these people aren't performing any extra or special service. They're just doing their job.

Tony S. of San Gabriel, CA, agrees. He asks, "Why should I tip someone who just hands me the money I've won? When I walk out the door after dropping $600 in the slots, does anyone come over and give me a tip?"

If you're losing or not doing anything special, no one expects you to tip. You don't tip for a hot slot that wasn't so hot. Tipping is for winners who want to tip.

And don't feel the more you win, the more you have to tip. Not so! For example, the next time you win $10,000, a 1% tip ($100) will do just fine.

What would you do in this situation? You're down $400 and hit a $1000 jackpot on a $1 Jeopardy slot. After your win is verified, a casino employee silently hands you nine $100 bills, four $20 bills, and one $10 bill. He then stands there looking at you, plainly expecting a tip. The implication being that you're petty and cheap if you don't.

Again, you should never feel obligated to tip unless a personal service has been performed (waitress, bellhop, keno runner, etc.). But, if the employee was courteous, friendly, and excited over your win, you might give him $10 or $20. Otherwise, just thank him with a smile and walk away.

To really s-t-r-e-t-c-h your money and playing time, try casino hopping. That is, play for a while at one casino, go to the one next door, then finish up at a third.

To keep you from spending all your time and money in one place, here are two suggestions:

(1) Set a loss limit for each casino. For example, in casino #1, play until you've lost $50, $100, $?. Then go to casino #2 and repeat.

(2) Set a time limit for each casino. Win or lose, you play for 30, 60, ? minutes, then move on. Setting predetermined goals like above keeps you in control of your emotions and bankroll at all times. A smart plan for any casino you play in.

Casino hopping not only adds fun and variety to your playing, but you'll also find that you have better luck at some casinos than at others.

If you ever get a special "hunch" or "feeling" about a particular machine, go for it. Mr. Spock of Star Trek fame may say it's highly illogical. But it's your feeling and your money. Besides, illogic is no stranger to the casino scene. For example:

GHOSTLY ADVICE

Betty Madewell of Longview, Texas spent several hours and a few hundred dollars playing slots at the Isle of Capri in Bossier City, La., when she decided it was time to head home. "I was sitting in my truck when something told me to go back in," she says. "It was my mom and I always believe she is watching over me when I win big."

With new confidence, she headed back into the casino and hit a $1,220,261 jackpot on a $5 IGT High Roller machine. When she saw the three High Roller symbols line up across the payline she nearly fainted. " I couldn't believe it, especially since I nearly walked out and left."

(CP September 1997)

The Real Lady Luck

Suzanne Henley is our pick for the "Luckiest Lady" in the world. You may not recognize her name, but we know you've heard her story. On Monday, April 14, at 1:47 a.m., Suzanne broke the world's record for the largest slot jackpot when she hit the Strip's newest megaresort, New York-New York.

Maybe it wasn't all luck. Suzanne says she had a feeling about that particular machine. "I had been to the casino a couple of times. The lines were so long, but after the first day, I told my hus-band which machine was going to win. It wasn't just picking—I had to play that machine. It was a physical feeling. Being around it almost made me ill. There was no question."

After waiting in line for an hour to play her machine, she sat down, plunked in the cash, and after 20 minutes, hit the biggest jackpot ever.

A local Las Vegan, Suzanne is continuing to work at her job as a construction inspector. Her husband is also still working, despite the fact that the couple will receive $500,000 annually for the next 20 years. They have bought a new house (and all new appliances), but have yet to make any other major purchases.

So why is she still working? The down-to-earth Suzanne simply says, "It's difficult to up and quit. Then what? How many days can you fish? How much time can I spend in the mall? You just don't need 10 closets full of stuff."

We asked Suzanne to share some of her favorite picks with us. Who knows... maybe some of her luck will rub off!

(CP August 1997)

Reprinted with permission from *Casino Player* Magazine.

A final word on feelings. It's OK to take an occasional fling at a slot based on a special hunch or feeling. It may add a little fun and excitement to your playing. But the key word is occasional. A feeling is no substitute for common sense. Trust it completely only when it tells you to stop. Then do so!

Then there's this *true* story about a player who was down to her last two dollars on a two-coin dollar slot. Before playing them off, she waved her arms over the slot, chanting "Booga, booga, booga." The result: a $1200 jackpot!

So even if you don't believe in magical incantations, when you're down to rock bottom, what have you got to lose? Booga, booga, booga!

Do you know why a slot attendant asks you to put in a coin to erase the winning symbols of a jackpot you've just won? You really don't have to. It's just considered casino etiquette. But if the attendant puts in a coin and hits another jackpot, it's the house's money, not yours.

If you'd like to reserve a machine for a restroom or other type of break, press the CHANGE button. The change person who responds will tell you how long it can be reserved for you. It's called capping. In most casinos, a floor person can cap a slot for up to two hours — depending on the player, the machine, and how busy the casino is. As a rule, a casino won't cap the superslots like Megabucks, Quartermania, etc.

Don't hesitate to ask a change person or slot attendant about their casino's capping policy. They'll be glad to accommodate you if they can. It builds goodwill and customer loyalty to the casino.

No matter how little a slot gives you back, it's called a win. In reality, the slot is just giving you back a little of what you put into it. Unless, of course, you hit a really big jackpot. But if you put $50 into a slot and got back $30, you didn't win $30, you lost $20. Simple math.

It's a fact that casinos have no clocks. The theory is that if you don't know what time it is, you're less likely to stop playing to get something to eat or sleep. It's a colorful theory. But the next time you're in a casino, notice how many players walk around with a clock on their wrists.

Need change? You no longer have to stand in line at the change booth or chase down a change person. It's simple. Just insert a bill into a slot's bill acceptor. Then when the appropriate amount of credits registers in the credit meter, hit the CASH/CREDIT button. Put the change that drops into the tray into a coin cup. Try not to play with coins lying in the tray. With a coin cup, you can see and feel how much you're winning or losing.

To entice people to come and play in their casino, some casinos trumpet THE LOOSEST SLOTS IN TOWN — implying that you have a better chance of winning there. But in many cases, it's mostly Madison Avenue hype, with honeyed words and heady promises. In Las Vegas, it's called a snow job in the desert.

However, casinos off the touristy path that advertise themselves as "local" or "neighborhood" casinos do tend to offer better-paying slots. Tourists are not their main market. To survive, they must generate a loyal customer base from people who live nearby.

These are the "locals." Residents who live within a five mile radius of the casino — players who are more interested in looser slots than in headliner shows and exotic themed attractions (pirates, erupting volcano, white tigers). So to attract and hold the local market, the casino offers slots with higher percentage paybacks and more frequent payouts.

So should you see or hear of a casino that boldly proclaims LOCALS PLAY HERE or WHERE LOCALS BRING THEIR FRIENDS, it might be worth checking out.

♠♠♠♠

Money and time management. In a casino, it makes good sense to think about how you're going to spend your time and money. If you plan a weekend getaway or three-day minivacation at a gaming resort destination like Atlantic City, Las Vegas, etc., here's a practical suggestion. Split each day into three playing sessions, with each session followed by some type of nongaming or break activity. For example:

AM
2-3 hr session + activity

PM
2-3 hr session + activity

EVE
2-3 hr session + activity

— BREAK ACTIVITY —

Shop, stroll, play keno or bingo, eat lunch or dinner, nap, read, watch TV in room, take in lounge or feature show, see "must-see" attraction, take a tour, visit another casino, relax by or take a dip in the pool, walk along the beach, schmooze with casino personnel, whale watch, etc.

Set a loss goal or limit for each session. For example, play until you've lost $50, $100, $?. Or set a time limit for each session. Win or lose you play for 2, 3, ? hours, then take a break.

To avoid slot combat fatigue, keep your playing sessions short. Two hours is the suggested maximum playing time without a break. Jabbing at buttons or pulling handles for clockless hours not only invites carpal tunnel syndrome, it wreaks havoc with your ability to think. And a frazzled mind becomes easily discouraged and leads to foolish, careless playing. So keep it short!

Try to strike a balance between gambling and relaxing. If you do, you'll feel better and play better. And see if you don't even win more often! Timely tip. Since casinos don't have clocks, bring your own!

With today's high-tech computerized slots, it's theoretically possible to program a computer chip to create a make-believe reel (virtual reel) as if there were hundreds, even thousands of symbols per reel. Meaning that your grandchildren, great-children and great-great-grandchildren could play the same slot around the clock, seven days a week, and not hit the top jackpot until some time in the next ice age. On a four-reel virtual slot, for example, there could be as many as 4,294,967,296 reel symbol combinations!

The term "change girl" is not only politically incorrect, in some cases it's downright wrong. More and more casinos are using men in the coin-dispensing role. Harrah's Las Vegas, for one. The politically correct casinospeak for a coin-dispenser (male or female) is change person or change attendant. A security guard is a security officer. A slot attendant is a floor person. Floor sweepers are porters or cleaning specialists. Cocktail waitresses are cocktail servers. Bartenders (male or female) are still called bartenders.

Fool's gold. You'd be surprised at the number of people who fall for this scam. Some fellow comes up to you and says that a slot mechanic friend of his has fixed a machine to pay off big. And for just $20 he'll take you to the fixed machine. It's all done with great mystery and secrecy. And after you've been ushered to the "rigged" machine and hand over your money, off goes the tipster. Of course, the obvious question to ask the tipster is that if he's on to such a sure thing, why doesn't he play it himself?

Have you played one of those coin-free slots that pay off non-taxable wins in credit tokens or customized casino scrip (voucher, ticket)? In the August 1999 edition of *Strictly Slots* magazine, readers were asked to pick the version of coin-free or cashless wagering they would most likely accept in their favorite casino: tokenization, ticket printers, cashless operation, or bill/scrip dispensers.

46

Of the 1,039 readers who responded, 897 (89%) said they want nothing to do with slot machines if actual coins are not involved. They would miss the fun of seeing and hearing coins dropping into the tray.

Whether coin-free slots or cashless wagering will be accepted by the majority of slot players is still being debated in the industry. But coin machines are here to stay. At least for the forseeable future.

♠♠♠♠

If you ever have the good fortune to hit the Big One, take immediate steps to protect your privacy. Start by refusing to have your picture taken. There's no requirement that your picture be taken before you are paid.

Here's the sad saga of a big winner who allowed a photo of him holding a giant cardboard check to be posted on the casino's winner wall and printed in national magazines and tabloids:

> *"I was pestered for months on end with phone calls from charities, salesmen, flimflam artists, curiosity seekers, and long-lost and not-so-long-lost friends and relatives. Spammers and scammers flooded my e-mail and "snail mail" boxes with all kinds of junk-mail offers: real estate deals, get-rich-quick schemes, marriage proposals, etc. And unwanted visitors and neighbors kept dropping by my home at all hours of the day and night. I ended up getting an unlisted phone number three times, renting a P.O. box, and taking a long, long, vacation."*

Self Defense. Get an unlisted phone number, a P.O. box, and an answering machine to screen all calls. Consult an estate-planning attorney, and hire a fee-only financial consultant to help you spend your money wisely. You might also call the Impact Project, Eugene, OR (1-800-255-4903), a group that offers free advice on how to handle major inheritances and large gambling winnings.

Avoid press conferences. And decline any requests for radio or TV appearances or any other activity that puts you in the harsh glare of the public spotlight. On November 15, 1998, a 67-year-old regular at the Palace Station in Las Vegas was the winner of a $27,582,539 Megabucks jackpot. Wisely, the stunned winner chose to remain anonymous. She spoke to reporters from behind a curtain and asked to be known simply as "Mrs. Lucky." Smart move, Mrs. Lucky.

Double-or-Nothing Betting Option (Wheel of Gold). On a slot with a double-or-nothing feature (also called "double up"), you have the option of doubling a winning payout by selecting the double-or-nothing button. Neither you nor the house has the advantage on this bet. Your chances of winning are 50-50 on each try. An even bet. But not a smart one.

Here, you're not risking just the few coins of a normal bet, but all the money you've already won! A chancy proposition. But if you insist, and only a small amount is involved, try the option once. Maybe twice. More than twice, you're not just pushing your luck, you're shoving it!

The STOP REELS feature. This feature lets you stop the reels at any point in their spin — even the instant they start spinning. There's really no need to watch the reels spin, since the computer has selected your win-loss symbol combination the moment you pulled the handle or pressed the spin button. By stopping the reels, you just learn sooner whether you've won or lost. *Bottom line*. Use this feature only if you're in a hurry or want lightning-speed play.

For all practical purposes, the handle on today's slot machine is a useless appendage. When you pull the handle and let go, it's the same as hitting the spin button. Ed Rogich, an executive director of International Game Technology, largest slot manufacturer in the world, said that the slot machine will always be made with a handle. Players just like to pull them. It's the only reason.

The millennial slot? In connection with its *Star Trek: The Experience* attraction, The Las Vegas Hilton Spacequest Casino features a number of slots with no handles or spin buttons.

The machines just have a device with a gap of two inches. When a player places his hand in the gap, it breaks a beam, causing the machine to play in the normal manner.

It's been reported that some people eke out a living strolling up and down casino aisles looking for coins left in a slot tray or on the floor. It's called silvermining or claiming. But whatever the name, the casino considers it theft, and the practitioner is subject to arrest.

There's really no harm in picking up an occasional coin or token you see lying on the floor. But [surprise} it's illegal for you to play with or remove coins from the tray or play off the credits on an unattended slot!

Here's why. A casino is private property. And all lost or unclaimed coins or tokens belong to the casino. A casino executive explained it this way: It's like visiting someone else's home. If you find money on the floor of that home, it's the homeowner's — not yours!

So as a good casino citizen, if you see an unattended slot with credits in the meter or coins in the tray, you should just walk on by or notify casino security or a slot floor person — as cleanup personnel are required to do.

You could, of course, return the money to the casino by putting it back into a slot. But what if you hit a big jackpot? Then you'd find some way of showing the casino your gratitude. Wouldn't you?

Occasionally a casino will advertise that some of its slots pay back 100% or more, the "teaser" slots. But when you enter that casino, there's no way to identify them.

The slot pros and "locals" eventually find these "come-on" slots and milk them for all they're worth. However, once the casino catches on, it resets the slots to pay back a lower percentage, and sets different machines to pay back the high percentage.

FREE SLOT PLAY. Here's another trick the casinos use to lure patrons into their establishment. Under the watchful eye of a casino employee, you're allowed one free pull at a special slot.

The prize won, if any, is of little value. A cheap trinket or casino logo item. Your chances of hitting the top prize at one of these free-pull machines are about as good as winning a free trip to the moon in the year 2099!

The moment you step away from a machine you've been playing, you've abandoned it. It's no longer yours. So if you leave a slot with the intention of coming back to it only to find it taken, it's too bad. You should have reserved it. To find out how, just summon a change person. They'll explain the casino's policy. Usually, a machine can be reserved for up to two hours.

The same rule applies if you start playing a slot and someone comes over to you and claims you're playing his machine. He says he just stepped away for a few moments. Don't be bullied or intimidated. It's your machine. Just tell the person very politely to reserve the machine the next time. Remember, you're in the right. And should the other party create a disturbance by using obnoxious language or behavior, press the CHANGE button to summon a change person. They in turn will contact a security officer.

Should you find a purse or wallet, don't turn it over to casino security. The latter will try to locate the owner, but if unsuccessful, the item reverts to the casino.

Better yet, check the purse or wallet for some ID. Then page the owner. If no response, call the hotel registration desk on the house phone to see whether the owner is a guest of the hotel.

If not, take the item to the local police department with a note that if the item isn't claimed, you wish to receive it. You're not only performing a good deed, there may be a reward in it for you.

♠♠♠♠

Slugs and foreign coins. If while cashing out, foreign coins or slugs drop into the tray, take them to the change booth or cashier's cage. If just a few pieces are involved, they'll give you the proper coin or token of the specific denomination. If more than just a few foreign coins or slugs drop into the tray, a full investigation is made of the machine.

♠♠♠♠

Did you ever wonder why Caesars Palace is not spelled Caesar's Palace? A casino's representative explained why. The casino created a Roman theme to make it appear that guests were walking into a Roman palace. And all its employees are trained to treat each guest with the respect and honor due a Caesar. In short, every guest is a Caesar. So Caesars is used as a plural descriptive adjective, not a possessive. A further example: The winners circle.

♠♠♠♠

A true incident. A man and his wife were playing slots in a major Las Vegas Strip casino. Their luck was phenomenal, and they were really raking it in. Until, that is, a shift boss came over to them and politely asked them to leave the casino.

"Why?" demanded the husband.

"Because," said the shift boss, "we think you're professional players and would rather you not play here."

Similar incidents have been reported by players in casinos throughout the country. When cashing in their winnings, they were told not to return. The casinos here hated the idea of losing money to a pro or to a smart player. And since it's hard to tell a smart player from just a lucky one, they take no chances.

The author queried a number of figures in the gaming industry and was told that the above were isolated incidents. Barring or expelling players who just happen to be luckier than average does not reflect general casino industry practice.

Like any other business, a casino is private property, and asking unwelcome patrons (drunks, troublemakers, etc.) to leave is perfectly legal. If they refuse or put up a struggle, they can be arrested for trespassing.

If for whatever reason you're asked to leave a casino, just do so. But don't show any physical ID (driver's license, slot club card, etc.) if asked. You are not required to show your ID to any casino employee unless you win $1200 or more on a single jackpot and must fill out IRS tax form W-2G.

Bottom line. If you've done nothing illegal, a casino can't stop you from leaving or detain you. But if they don't want your business, they can legally ask you to leave. It's called being 86'd. And should you be read the trespass act while being led to an exit, you can be arrested if you return.

Machine malfunction. When you play a slot machine or video game, you enter into a contract with the casino. The payout table (or "glass") on top of the machine spells out the coin payout for various symbol combinations. An important element of the contract is the message on the glass saying "Malfunction voids all pays and plays." Or something to that effect.

After a big jackpot hit, slot personnel routinely open up the slot to be sure it hasn't been tampered with and that the slot's computer program is working properly. They then compare the computer's electronic record of the game against the symbol combination displayed on the reels.

If the symbol combination on the reels doesn't match the electronic record of the game, a malfunction is declared and the jackpot is denied. It's the computer's electronic record of the game that is considered the actual outcome. Not what's displayed on the reels.

In Nevada, the Gaming Control Board ruled that in case of a malfunction, the player is entitled to receive only a refund of the wager made on the voided play. Should you wish to dispute a Nevada casino's claim of a malfunction or incorrect payout, insist on getting everything documented: the time, date, place, names of witnesses, casino personnel, etc.

If the amount of the dispute is over $500, the casino must notify the Enforcement Division of the Nevada Gaming Control Board. If the amount is under $500, you can ask the casino to phone the Enforcement Division (open 24 hours a day) so you can speak with an agent. If it refuses, ask for the phone number and make the call yourself. Just don't leave. Make the call from the casino.

In New Jersey, the Casino Control Commission has a resident agent in each casino — available 24-hours a day.

The computer chips in today's slots have a memory of at least the last three or four games played — including how many coins were inserted, when played, and the win-loss symbols that came up. Evidence that's hard to dispute.

Every casino, no matter where located, is subject to some type of state gaming control. So if you wish to make a claim or complaint against a casino, contact the applicable state gaming authority.

Many players claim they know how to play slots, but just don't know when to quit. The most obvious time, of course, is when you run out of money. Other times are when playing is no longer fun because you're tired, upset, hungry, depressed, sleepy, desperate, and when arms and fingers become sore.

If you keep playing when emotionally and physically drained, you're asking for trouble. And the casino is always willing and able to provide it.

Casinos rarely put loose slots next to or even near one another. So if you're lucky enough to find a loose slot, you can bet that the slots on either side of it are going to be tight. So when winning, it's best to play only one slot at a time. If you play the slots on either side of it, you'll just be putting your winnings back into tight machines.

And if you're playing with a spouse or friends, don't let them sit at the slot next to you...or even near you! But even tight slots pay out eventually. That's why you may see a player hitting on three slots right next to one another. A rare event! But one which proves that slot playing is absolutely unpredictable, uncontrollable, unfathomable. ANYTHING CAN HAPPEN - AT ANY TIME!

However, it's still best to play just one slot at a time. It stretches your playing time. But if you like to play more than one, play only as many as you can keep in sight at all times. Casinos have two-armed bandits too. Read on.

 **"Casino Quotes"**

Bad luck isn't all bad. It's what keeps casinos in business.

A wonderfully consoling thought about losing at slots is that when you look around, you'll always see someone who's doing worse.

The casinos' emphasis on being a place of fun and entertainment is to encourage their patrons who feel bad about losing to feel good about it.

Money won at gambling can't buy happiness. But losing can't buy anything.

The Casino - a place where nothing ventured, nothing lost.

9

SOME BASIC DO'S AND DON'TS

DON'T be confused or intimidated by a casino's electronic wonderland of live-action video slots with their gimmicky names (Top Dog, Moo Money), computer-animated cartoon characters (pigs, cows, fish) and digital sound and musical effects.

There's a great mystique surrounding today's high-tech computerized slots. But like cloned sheep, all slots are basically alike. They're simply a cabinet housing the slot's hardware and software produced by the manufacturer. And they all work on the same principle. You put in one or more coins and wait to see what Lady Luck (a tiny computer chip) has in store for you.

DON'T feed bills into the slot's bill acceptor ($1-$100) to buy gaming credits. Some players claim it's a practical way to keep track of their bankroll and the slot's ups and downs. But when you play with credits, money loses all meaning. You don't think of those little numbers in the credit meter as real money. They're more like psychological pain killers that soften the pain of losing. Somehow, losing 400 credits on a quarter slot doesn't seem so bad as losing $100.

Casinos know that when people play with coins, they tend to flit from slot to slot. But when they play with credits, most will stay with one slot, playing the wins in the credit meter down to zero. They also tend to play longer and make bigger bets. It may be tiresome to hand-feed coins into a slot (and few players do). But when you hold a bucketful of coins in your hands, you can easily see and feel how much you're winning or losing.

Playing with coins also forces you to slow down — which extends your playing time and bankroll. And the more mileage you can squeeze out of your bankroll, the longer you can play. Try this. Play for a while with credits. Then for a while with coins. See if you don't feel and play differently when you have real money in your hands.

DON'T be tricked into staying at a slot by the "near miss" feature. This is when you keep seeing the winning symbols lined up just above or below the payline or partially on the payline, like 7-7-bar. Naturally, you think you just missed by a hair, and it's a sign that the next spin or two will do the trick. Right? Wrong! Winning symbols will occasionally appear like this, but simply as a result of the computer's random selection process. You notice them merely because they show up so infrequently. It doesn't increase or decrease your likelihood of winning. It just tricks you into playing longer.

One Nevada-based slot manufacturer actually built the "near miss" feature into his slot's computer programming, claiming that it made the game more fun and exciting for the player. But the state gaming regulators didn't agree and told him to remove it.

In reality, there's no such thing as a "near miss" in slot playing. It falls into the category of "due" or "bound to hit" described on page 11.

DO leave home without them: your checkbook, ATM card, debit card, and the galaxy of credit cards crammed in your wallet. Take just one credit card and use it for out-of-pocket expenses only: meals, shows, shopping, etc. This lessens the urge to splurge and the risk of maxing out your VISA or cleaning out your bank account.

And beware of a new, insidious trick some casinos are introducing to take your hard-earned money. The card swipe. This is a device attached to a slot that lets you swipe your credit or debit card. With a credit card, you give the slot direct access to your credit card balance. With a debit card, you give it direct (and usually immediate) access to your checking or savings account. *Bottom line.* Credit in a casino is a fancy name for trouble.

Another wallet-emptying gambit in the casino's bag of tricks is "cashless" slot playing. Here the player deposits funds into a casino-held account for slot play. When he's ready to play, the player swipes an account access card through the card reader on the slot, electronically transferring credits from his account to the slot machine.

And steer clear of the casino-brand credit cards and those ubiquitous ATMs. Playing with plastic will come back to haunt you when the bank statements start coming in.

Bottom line: Play only with the money you bring to the casino. Bring it in cash. And play only with this cash. When it's gone, your playing is over. Go home or do something different to take your mind off gambling.

If you bring a really large amount of money, traveler's checks are a safe option.

DON'T drink alcoholic beverages while gambling. Casinos know that alcohol loosens a player's inhibitions, and the purse strings soon follow. If thirsty, get a glass of water from the bar (free). Or ask a cocktail server to bring you a soft drink. Suggested tip: 50¢.

DO read carefully the payout table of any slot you're not familiar with. If you have trouble understanding it, get help. Ask a nearby player or press the CHANGE button. The change person who responds may be able to help you. If not, they'll summon a slot attendant who can. Explaining how slots work is part of their job. And they'll be glad to help you. Don't be afraid to ask. And no, you don't have to tip. Unless you want to.

DON'T play more than one slot at a time. Here's why: (1) You speed up your play — which means you bet more and lose faster. (2) You're vulnerable to thieves who look for players playing more than one machine, the tray dippers. While one thief distracts you in some way, his accomplice grabs a fistful of coins from the unwatched tray(s). (3) When betting max coin at a 3-coin slot, you may not notice that all lights or lines are lit, or that a coin dropped straight through to the tray. So you're playing with two coins when you think you're playing with three.

And as mentioned elsewhere, casinos rarely put "loose" slots next to or even near one another! So if you play more than one slot, you're guaranteed to be playing at least one "tight" one.

DON'T play in any casino that's so crowded you have only a limited selection of slots to choose from. If you can't "slot hop" or have to stand in line to wait your turn to play, go to another casino — or try to play when there's less of a crowd (midweek, early a.m., late p.m.). Also, avoid visiting casinos on weekends and holidays with their endless lines and bone-crushing crowds.

Then there's the special-effects Clint Eastwood slot.
You drop in a coin and a disembodied voice says,
"Let me make your day."

The Sheepish Credit Manager

A man returns to his hotel room after asking the casino credit manager for a line of credit. His wife asks, "Well, dear, did you get a line of credit?"
Husband: "Why, that credit manager was just like a lamb."
Wife: "Really? What did he say?"
Husband: "Ba-a-a-a-a-h!"

A. *"I have absolutely no luck with slots. I'm giving them up."*
B. *"Lucky fellow."*

Math teacher to gambler's son: *"If your father had $300 and a friend asked him for a loan of $200, how much would your father have left?*
Gambler's son: "Three hundred dollars."

"You're cheating!" *the card dealer said to one of the players.*
"No, I'm not!" the player said.
"You must be," said the dealer.
"You're not playing the cards I dealt you."

During WWII *some GIs were playing poker in a British pub with some of the local men. One of the British players picked up his hand and said, "I'll wager a pound." A GI looked at his hand, which had four aces. He said, "I don't know much about your money, but I'll see you a pound and raise you a ton."*

10

WHY YOU NEED A STRATEGY

Fully 90% of the players you see at any one time on the slot floor have no idea what they're doing. They simply select a slot at random, plunk in their money and hope for the best. Players whom Frank Sinatra, one-time owner of the Cal-Neva casino in Lake Tahoe, referred to as "wall-to-wall losers."

Through sheer dumb luck and the help of friendly angels they may win now and then, but get greedy and wind up putting it all back in. When they run out of money, they walk away, chalking it all up to fun — players the casinos dub "happy losers." But guess who's really having all the fun!

Playing with a strategy means that you're using some kind of pattern or plan, rather than playing randomly. A strategy won't change the house odds, but it helps keep your losses down, extends your playing time, and gives you better control over your emotions and bankroll.

Surveys in player psychology showed that players with a strategy tend to do better than those without one. The players also reported a more satisfying and less frustrating casino experience.

The basic playing strategy shown for the various denomination slots on the following pages is perhaps one of the most practical and least expensive ways to play. It has proven itself on the casino floor and in extensive mathematical and computer testing at a leading West Coast university.

Work with it for a while. Then ignore it. It was designed mainly for you to use as a guide to tailor a strategy that works best for you.

It really doesn't matter what strategy you devise. Just as long as you use it consistently. This doesn't mean using it now and then. Or constantly changing or trashing it when it doesn't seem to work. It means sticking to it no matter what happens at any playing session or on any given day! Give it a good chance to work before changing it.

The one big advantage of playing by a strategy is that it slows you down. You're forced to think about what you're doing. And this takes time — which lengthens your bankroll and playing time. The true secret of modern slot playing.

Sadly, not everyone has the patience and self-discipline to devise and work with a strategy. They're trapped in a tight little comfort zone of habits and attitudes that keeps them from trying anything new. As Yogi Berra would say, "If people don't want to change their playing habits, you can't stop them."

One slot aficionado from CA cheerily dismissed the whole strategy idea with "I don't go to a casino to think. I just go to have a good time." The type of player the casinos just love down to the last dollar.

—Old Gambler's Saying———
"Any strategy is better than no strategy."

The Invisible Man
Q. "Why was the Invisible Man depressed?"
A. "He won $2000 at roulette. But because he had no photo ID, they wouldn't pay him."

Today's slots *really have some unique names. There's one called FLATTERY. It gets you nowhere. Then there's one called ENTHU-SIASM. Everybody puts everything they've got into it."*

Teacher to a gamber's son: *"Billy, you should never underrate yourself. You know what underrate means, don't you?"*
Gambler's son: "Yes, teacher. Seven and under."

Waiter to customer *in a casino restaurant. "Would you like your coffee black, sir?"*
Customer: "What other colors do you have?"

Wife to husband: *"How many times have I told you not to throw your money away on slots?"*
Husband: "I don't know. I thought you were keeping score."

11
SET A WIN GOAL

We've all heard it a zillion times: Quit while you're ahead. Good advice. And easy to do for some, but impossible for others.

It's not hard to win at slots. It's just hard to keep from putting it all back in. That's why the most common mistake slot players make is to play and replay all winnings until they go broke. Each win merely whets their appetite for more. They're sure the next spin will do the trick. In short, they get greedy and put it all back in.

If you ever hope to go home with some (or a lot) of the casino's money in your pocket, you must learn to set aside part of your winnings. Call it a **win goal.**

How much? That's up to you. Just make it a habit to put aside some of each win to take home. Savvy slot players convert part or all of their wins into big bills ($20s, $50s, $100s) and tuck them away in a remote corner of their wallet or purse. You don't spend what you don't see. And it's one of the smartest ways of managing your money.

So before you set foot in a casino, ask yourself three simple questions:

1) Do I keep all session winnings?

2) Do I replay all session winnings?

3) Do I keep some of each session's winnings and play with the rest?

If you answer yes to number 3), how much would it take in winnings to satisfy you? 25%, 50%, 75%? In other words, if you won $100, would you keep $25, $50, $75? Whatever amount you choose, that's your win goal for the session. And that's what you're going to cash in, put in your wallet, and take home.

It's that simple. And by setting your win goal in advance, you'll remain calm and in emotional control no matter what happens. No hassle by other players. No hasty on-the-spot decisions in the excitement of winning. You're always in control and ready and able to deal with anything that happens.

In her book "The Frugal Gambler," Jean Scott says that the first step to clear thinking in a casino is to recognize that gambling is a recreational activity. The goal is, or should be, entertainment.

So don't go into a casino with the idea of making money. As Steve Wynn, chairman of Mirage Resorts, said, "The only way to make money in a casino is to own one."

Your goal should be small but consistent wins. They keep you playing longer and give you the fun and excitement you're looking for. Just remember to play slowly, keep your bets low, and put some of each win aside — no matter how small. You may not come home with much money. But at least you'll come home a winner more often.

A "local" in Las Vegas said he plays with a daily bankroll of $50 and keeps $1 of each win. A small win goal, but one that guarantees he always walks out of the casino with some money.

> *Old Gambler's Saying*
> *"Bad luck never lasts forever.*
> *It continues for a while — then gets worse!"*

————————— **"Casino Quotes"** —————————

The casinos just love their slot club members. They're a credit to their cards.

The casinos think of everything. They now make it possible for anyone who wants to win big in the worst possible way to do so. It's called BET MAX COIN.

Sign above entrance to casino in Puerto Rico: SE HABLA YOUR BANKROLL.

12

CASINO SECURITY AND THEFT

Although casino security is generally good, each casino has its share of coin scoopers, wallet lifters, purse snatchers, coin-rack pilferers, and coin cup grabbers. And the last thing you want to do is share your winnings with a thief.

Usually working in teams (all sexes, ages, races), petty grab-and-run thieves prowl the slot aisles sizing up potential victims. Their target of choice is a man or woman age 50 on up and playing alone. But it could be anyone they think might be easily distracted or not paying attention.

Waiting for the right moment, they approach the victim and distract him/her in a perfectly normal way: asking for the time, spilling a drink, pretending to trip, etc. A common ploy is to throw coins on the floor near the victim's slot and say something like "Hey, lady! You're spilling coins all over the floor." When the victim looks down, the thief's accomplice grabs a handful of coins from the tray, a coin rack, a bucketful of coins, or a purse lying on the floor.

Then there's the tray dipper (aka till tapper) — a penny-ante thief who helps himself to the coins or tokens in someone else's tray. In one scenario, the tray dipper looks for a player playing two or more machines, with coins lying in the tray of each. Pretending to play a machine nearby, he waits for the player to look away from a machine, then snatches a few coins from the unwatched tray.

In another scenario, the tray dipper sits at a slot next to the target player and pretends to play. The moment the target looks away from his slot, the dipper reaches over and grabs a few coins or tokens. But not so many that the victim notices.

A variant approach to tray dipping is the "distract team." Here a team of two thieves sits at opposite sides of the targeted player. While one thief distracts the player in some way, the other snatches a fistful of coins or tokens from the tray and scoots off.

Should you catch a tray dipper in the act, you can respond in any number of ways. But the recommended way is simply to tell the dipper quietly, but firmly, to put the money back.

Dippers aren't the nicest people in the world and can get really nasty when caught. It's not worth making a big scene over a few coins or tokens and spoiling your trip.

But being a good casino citizen, there's one thing you can do, if you wish. Let's say the dipper puts the money back and leaves. Follow him quietly. If he hangs around the casino, tell a security officer what happened. If you're in a major casino, an overhead video surveillance camera will have recorded the incident.

According to the Nevada Gaming Control Board, tray dipping is considered petty theft and is a misdemeanor. The dipper is subject to arrest, but only if the victim prefers charges. If not, the dipper is read the trespass act by casino security and escorted to an exit. If he returns, he is subject to arrest for trespassing.

This is all the action the casino takes, since it's the player's money that's involved — not the casino's.

In Nevada, however, cheating, stealing, or any other type of criminal activity involving casino money is considered a gaming–related crime and a felony — whether the amount is $5 or $5000.

Punishment depends on many factors. A first offender faces up to six years in prison and/or a $10,000 fine, or may be put on probation. If a previous offender is caught again, he's guaranteed a suite in a Nevada state facility overlooking the exercise yard.

Far more common than tray dipping is purse snatching (#1 casino theft) and coin-bucket filching (#2 casino theft).

Should you become the victim of some type of nongaming criminal activity while on casino property (assault, mugging, robbery, etc.), it's a matter for the local police. And if you feel that the casino isn't handling the matter to your satisfaction, phone the police yourself. The casino doesn't have the last word in a non-gaming related crime.

If the incident took place in a major casino, it will be recorded on an overhead video surveillance camera. And the police have the right to enter the casino and confiscate the tape for examination.

Jackpot Hijacking. The security head of a major Las Vegas casino was asked about jackpot highjacking. This is where, conditions being right, one member of a team of two thieves will push a jackpot winner aside and claim the win. And in the ensuing fracas, the hijacker's accomplice backs up the claim. This is considered robbery and is a felony.

However, the security head mentioned that the highjacking scene described above would be extremely unlikely in today's casinos. All slot machines in major casinos are under constant video camera surveillance, and the tape would clearly show who the original player was and everything that happened thereafter.

Below are some common-sense steps you can take to protect yourself and your money in a casino. They're not meant to scare you, since a casino has ample security, backup, and plain clothes personnel to handle any type of situation.

They're just to remind you that every casino has its share of unsavory characters skilled in ripping off inattentive and unwary players. Just knowing that these characters exist will make you less likely to be victimized.

1. Don't flash around your wallet, credit cards, or large amounts of money. When checking in at an upscale casino/ hotel, ask whether there's a safe if your room. If not, ask the check-in clerk about the use of a safe deposit box. Use of the box is free and is accesible 24 hours a day. All hotels encourage their use. It's a good idea, especially if you're carrying a large amout of money.

2. Should you hit a win in the thousands and don't want to carry the cash around, ask the cashier whether you can be paid by casino check. As a rule, casinos don't like to issue checks. But they will in some cases, if asked. It usually depends on the amount of the win.

   And to eliminate the danger of being attacked by a mugger, don't hesitate to ask for an escort to a safe deposit box, to your room, or to your car in the parking lot. Casinos will gladly provide an escort if asked.

3. In a crowded elevator, casino aisle, check-in line, show-line, etc., it's not unusual to have people bumping into you. And one of these human fender benders could be a pick-pocket. Here's how to thwart them:

   Men: To keep your wallet from being lifted, carry it in your shirt pocket or put a rubber band around it.

   Ladies: To keep your purse from being stolen, don't carry one. Wear a fanny pack instead. They're inexpensive, and most casino gift shops sell them. If you must take your purse with you, wrap the strap around your wrist or hang it around your neck while playing. Never, never place it on the floor between your feet or beside the slot!

4. Beware of the late-night hotel scam. The phone rings when you're asleep and sure to be groggy when awakened. The caller claims to be a staff member of the hotel and asks for your credit card number to verify their records or some other pretext. Hang up! Never give your credit card number over the phone.

   Bottom line. Be alert to the people and activity around you. The casino predators just love those slot potatoes so obsessed with the mindless exchange of coins with a machine that they wouldn't notice a white elephant sitting down and playing the slot next to them.

   A final tip. Be wary of shoulder-surfing nonplayers who lurk behind or near you. They may be innocent onlookers. Maybe not. But take no chances. If one of them approaches you for any reason, put your hand over any winnings. And resist the urge to be friendly. It's better to appear impolite than to be victimized.

13

THE IRS WINS TOO

Casinos must report all slot machine wins of $1200 or more on a single jackpot to the IRS, since gambling winnings are taxed as regular income. So if you win such an amount, you'll be asked to sign IRS Form W-2G (the G stands for gambling) and for your Social Security number and some photo ID (e.g., driver's license). Without the photo ID you won't get paid.

your silent partner

	☐ CORRECTED (if checked)		
PAYER'S name, address, ZIP code, Federal identification number, and telephone number	1 Gross winnings $1250	2 Federal income tax withheld ----	OMB No. 1545-0238
	3 Type of wager $1.00 slot	4 Date won 12; 22 ;99	1999
CASINO NAME AND ADDRESS	5 Transaction TBS	6 Race ----	Form W-2G
	7 Winnings from identical wagers ----	8 Cashier TBS	Certain Gambling Winnings
WINNER'S name, address (including apt. no.), and ZIP code	9 Winner's taxpayer identification no. ----	10 Window --;--	This is important tax information and is being furnished to the Internal Revenue Service. If you are required to file a return, a negligence penalty or other sanction may be imposed on you if this income is taxable and the IRS determines that it has not been reported.
YOUR NAME AND ADDRESS	11 First I.D. Soc. Security No.	12 Second I.D. Driver's License	
	13 State/Payer's state identification no. As applicable	14 State income tax withheld As applicable	
Under penalties of perjury, I declare that, to the best of my knowledge and belief, the name, address, and taxpayer identification number that I have furnished correctly identify me as the recipient of this payment and any payments from identical wagers, and that no other person is entitled to any part of these payments.			Copy C For Winner's Records
Signature ►		Date ►	
Form W-2G		Department of the Treasury - Internal Revenue Service	

As a rule, the casino won't withhold any taxes on a slot win (no matter what the amount) unless the winner is a nonresident alien or foreign corporation. Some casinos will withhold the tax if you ask them to (usually 28%). Policies vary.

The casino sends one copy of the Form W-2G to the IRS and gives you a copy. You do not have to attach your copy to your April 15 income tax form unless the casino withheld the tax for some reason. You just have to show what you won on the "Other Income" line of Form 1040.

A. CASINO LOSSES

The good news is that you can deduct all casino gaming losses up to the amount of the win — reported on Schedule A as "Other Miscellaneous Deductions." To substantiate your losses, you must be able to show the IRS (if audited) accurate, itemized records of casino wins and losses, but only in the year they occurred. Previous years' wins and losses don't count.

So if you feel lucky, take a pad or notebook to the casino with you, and keep a diary or similar record of your wins and losses (keno, bingo, slot machines, sports book, etc.). The diary should contain at least the following information:

* Date and type of wager
* Name and location of the casino
* Names of other persons (if any) present with you at the time
* Amount(s) you won or lost

And this is where membership in a casino slot club comes in handy. As a member, you can ask for a free year-end printout of your slot-playing wins and losses at that casino. But not every casino provides this service. You'll have to ask at the casino's Slot or Player's Club. If it does, just send it a signed request, with your name, address, telephone number, Social Security Number, and club card membership number. It could make an IRS audit less taxing.

According to a 1996 Tax Court ruling, the value of "comps" (complimentary awards, prizes, services) is considered to be gaming winnings and should be included in total winnings. When you ask a casino for a year-end printout of your slot-playing wins and losses, its accounting department will figure the value of any comps and add them to your total winnings.

Other casino-related gambling records required are:

* W-2Gs

* Wagering tickets or receipts

* Canceled checks

* Credit card records (ATM withdrawals)

* Bank withdrawals

* Any receipts provided by the casino.

Expenses incidental to gambling, such as meals, lodging, airfare, etc., are not deductible as losses. These classes of expenses are deductible only by professional gamblers and others who can show a direct business link, such as writers.

B. OTHER GAMBLING LOSSES

Losses from all other forms of gambling are also deductible up to the amount of the winnings. These include, but are not limited to:

* Sweepstakes	* Bingo	* Dog racing
* Lotto/lottery	* Jai alai	* Charity drawings/raffles
* Keno	* Horse racing	* Sports book

To substantiate your claim, be sure to keep all wagering tickets or receipts, canceled checks, credit card records (ATM cash advances), bank withdrawals, plus other evidence of wagering. Add the total wagering losses of A and B together and report as one figure on Schedule A, "Other Miscellaneous Deductions."

Married couples can combine their wins and losses for reporting purposes on all types of gambling, provided it's a joint return.

If you have a reportable win and substantial comps, it would be wise to check with a qualified tax accountant or tax preparer familiar with gaming tax law.

As a note of interest, some slots feature a top prize of $1,199 — just $1.00 below the $1,200 IRS reporting requirement.

Whoever said nothing is impossible never played slot machines.

An Apt Description

Guest of the Bellagio, the 1.8-billion-dollar hotel/casino on the Las Vegas Strip: "This is my kind of place. Simple but lavish."

A barker in a circus *offered a curious throng $100 if anyone could get another drop of juice out of a lemon after the circus strong man had squeezed it. Several men tried and failed. Finally a man came up and, after considerable effort, squeezed another drop of juice from the lemon.*

"Here's your $100," said the barker. "If you don't mind, sir, could you tell me how you did it?"

"Not at all," replied the man. "I'm the credit manager in a Reno casino."

A guest checked into *a Las Vegas motel and was getting ready for bed when he noticed a little book on the night table titled "The Bedside Companion." On the contents page was a list of articles to read for certain occasions. "If you are depressed and down in the dumps, read page 37. If you are lonesome and restless, read page 54." The man turned to page 54 and read the article. Then he noticed that someone had written at the bottom of the page in a feminine scrawl, "If you are still lonesome and restless, call AP 4-0987 and ask for Betty."*

Some of the off-the-strip *restaurants in Las Vegas will do anything to get more business. I visited one where they had topless waitresses. I'm against it. But my wife doesn't believe me.*

"You're against waitresses wearing topless outfits?" she asked incredulously.

"Sure am," I said. "It's bad enough when they put their fingers in your soup."

A. *"I hear they're looking for a casino cage cashier."*
B. *"Really? I thought they hired one a month ago."*
A. *"They did. That's the one they're looking for."*

14

WHAT OTHER PLAYERS DO

Below are some of the comments taken from a nationwide survey of slot players much like you. They offer a small spectrum of experiences from which you can put your own playing experiences in perspective. Note the player's win goal shown in bold type.

Maxine R.
Arcadia, CA

An occasional day-tripper to Laughlin and Las Vegas. *"I allot $125 for the day. Mostly for 25¢ slots. I never replay anything that drops into the tray.* **I keep all winnings!** *I always take with me a jade figurine of a Buddha which I picked up in Singapore. I know it sounds silly, but before each bet, I rub its tummy and say, 'Come on, Buddha baby!' It doesn't always work, unfortunately."*

Duncan B.
Bridgeport, CT

Day-tripper to Foxwoods and Mohegan Sun in CT. *"My playing budget for the day is $200. Play mostly $1 slots. Always play max coins for 4-5 pulls.* **Cash in and take home all wins $100 and over.** *Move down to 25¢ slots if bankroll goes down too fast. Play off all small wins."*

Mary P.
Sun City, AZ

Day-tripper to Las Vegas and Arizona Indian casinos. *"I go with $200-$300. And I play mostly quarter slots. Occasionally, I'll move up to the 2-coin dollar slots, playing max coins for about 10 pulls. Then move on if I don't win.* **I usually play off all wins under $200. I keep anything over this amount."**

Paul C. **Ontario, Canada**	Day-tripper to Canadian casinos in Windsor and Niagara Falls. *"My wife and I share a $100 bankroll for the day. We play mostly 25¢ slots. How I bet varies. Sometimes I bet just one coin; other times, max coins. It depends on the slot and how I feel."*
Bess C. **Pittsburgh, PA**	Las Vegas vacationer at the Stardust. *"My daily playing budget is $100. I play mostly quarter slots, maximum coins. Usually one roll per slot. I enjoy playing the slots. So I play off all winnings to extend my playing time."*
Isabelle C. **Pittsburgh, PA**	Bess's sister. *"My playing bankroll is $125 per day. I play 25¢ slots only.* ***I play off all wins up to $100 and keep the rest.*** *I stick to one slot the whole time I play. Don't like to move around. I'll stay at a slot as long as it keeps paying or until I get tired or run out of money."*
June Van H. **St. George, UT**	Day-tripper to Las Vegas and Mesquite, NV, casinos. *"I stick pretty much to the nickel slots. I always bet max coin, but drop down to just one coin if the game goes too fast. I tried some of those new nickel 5- to 9-line multi-coin slots, but didn't care too much for them. I couldn't figure out why I won what I did..*

WHAT'S <u>YOUR</u> WIN GOAL?

> *A psychologist said slot playing is a lot like sex.*
> *Both give you something to do with your hands.*

72

15
THE ROLE OF LUCK

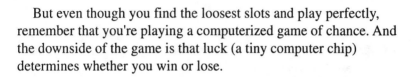

Strategy, money management, discipline. That's what this book is all about. And by following its common-sense tips and guidelines, you'll play with more confidence and have some control over what's going to happen. And the more elements you can control, the more luck you'll have.

But even though you find the loosest slots and play perfectly, remember that you're playing a computerized game of chance. And the downside of the game is that luck (a tiny computer chip) determines whether you win or lose.

So expect sessions or days when whatever strategy you use or whatever you do, nothing seems to go right. Even savvy professionals win no more than 30% of the time. And on some days they don't win at all!

But even losing has its positive side. It shows you what works and what doesn't. So the next time you'll know what to do and what not to do.

Remember: In slot playing, there's always mañana.

What is Luck?

"Luck is what happens when preparation meets opportunity."
— Louis Pasteur

"You can't hope to be lucky. You have to prepare to be lucky."
— Timothy Dowd, NYPD

"The harder I work, the more luck I have."
— Damon Runyon

"Luck is being at the right slot at the right time."
— Old Gambler's Saying

Heaven and the Casino Manager

Saint Peter was standing at the Pearly Gates greeting new arrivals. To one he said, "Welcome to heaven. And what did you do on earth?"

"I was a teacher," replied the new arrival.

Saint Peter said, "Welcome. We have a special place for you."

The next arrival said, "I was a minister."

St. Peter said, "Welcome. We have a very special place for you."

The next arrival said, "I was a casino manager."

Saint Peter said, "Welcome. We have a room for you. But you can stay only three days."

A deceased casino debt collector *knocked on the gates of hell and asked Satan for permission to enter. "Why do you wish to come in here?" asked Satan.*

Collector: "I just want to collect some gambling debts from welchers who died before I could collect."

Satan: "How do you know they're here?"

Collector: "Well, every time I tried to collect, this is the place everyone told me to go."

An inveterate slot *player presented herself at the Pearly Gates. St. Peter welcomed her and asked for her credentials. Opening her purse, she proudly showed her slot club membership cards for Ballys, MGM, the Venetian, Bellagio, and the Flamingo Hilton. She then showed pictures of herself shaking hands with Bugsy Siegel, Steve Wynn, and Ted Turner. St. Peter, impressed, said, "Come in, Madam, by all means. But I don't think you're going to like it here."*

Satan to pit boss: *"The trouble with you pit bosses is that you think you are the best people down here. Well, you're not. You're just the most numerous."*

A woman told a doctor friend *that every time she played slots for an hour she became dizzy. "But when the hour has passed, I feel OK. What do you recommend?"*

Doctor: "Play for only 59 minutes."

Suggested Playing Strategies

THE DOLLAR SLOT

The goal of the strategy below is to test as many 2-token, 3-reel, single-payline, nonprogressive dollar slots as possible until you find the right slot to play. Sticking to 2-token dollar slots will save you a lot of money.

To start:

1. Set a win goal per session ($25, $50, $?). The win amount you're going to cash in and take home.

2. Buy 2 rolls of dollar tokens ($40), or get tokens directly from the slot. Put the tokens into a coin cup. Don't play with tokens lying in the tray.

3. Select a carousel or bank of 2-token, 3-reel, single-payline, nonprogressive dollar slots *in an area of heavy traffic and visible from many directions on the casino floor!*

4. At slot #1, set a **test-spin** limit (4, 5, ? spins). Say 4 spins.

5. Insert **1 token** at a time for these 4 spins.

6. If you lose 4 times in a row, go to slot #2 and start over (**1 token**, 4, 5, ? spins).

7. If you get back just a few tokens or credits, play them off — also **1 token** at a time.

EXCEPTIONS TO ONE-TOKEN BET LIMIT. Here are four suggested times to bet max coin: at an in-house progressive, at a linked progressive (Megabucks), during a hot streak, and at a slot with a *guaranteed or certified* percentage payback.

8. If you start getting small but consistent wins or hit a hot streak, bet **2 tokens**. And stay at that slot as long as it keeps paying. When it stops, set a losing-spin limit and move on.

Bet 1 token to start, and set a firm test-spin limit!

77

SUGGESTED POST-WIN STRATEGY

The post-win strategy below was designed to be flexible. So feel free to change any figures or amounts to fit your particular bankroll or playing style. Do whatever works best for you.

SMALL TO MIDSIZE WINS ($50 to $500)

CAUTION: Don't get greedy! To greedy players, no win is ever enough. They want more. So they play and replay all tokens and credits — and go from being a sure winner to a sure loser. To walk away a winner, do the following:

Just one More!

* Set aside the amount of the win goal (take-home money) you established for each session. Keep HALF of the rest of the win to shop, take in a show, pay trip expenses, etc. Use the other half to play with. Try to keep at least half of all wins thereafter.

* Now, increase your bets to **2 tokens** per spin. (Rule: double up only after a sizable win. Don't count the return of a few coins as a win.)

* Keep betting **2 tokens** per spin as long as you're winning.

* The instant you sense or realize that you're no longer winning, set a firm losing-spin limit — no more than 5 to 10 spins!

* If you reach this losing-spin limit, stop playing! Not one extra pull! Setting losing-spin limits will keep you playing during a hot streak and will warn you when a cold streak has begun.

When no longer winning, set a firm losing-spin limit.
And stick to it!

BIG WIN (over $500)

IMPORTANT: After a big win, make sure that the figure in the WINNER PAID meter agrees with the figure shown for that particular win combination in the payout table. If it doesn't, the machine probably ran out of money or jammed. If this happens, the light on top of the machine will blink to summon an attendant. A figure like 3200 or 3300 will also appear in the credit meter. It's called the tilt code.

* Depending on the amount of the win, the payout may be made entirely by the slot (cash, voucher) or in part or full by an attendant.

* When part or all of the payout is to be made by an attendant, a light on top of the slot will blink, or the slot will make some kind of sound (loud ring or musical tone) to summon the attendant.

* Until the attendant arrives, don't leave, touch or take your eyes off the slot for any reason. Big cash winners make big targets for the ever-present casino thieves.

* If the slot blacks out during a payout, it's probably due to a malfunction, coin jam, or it simply ran out of coins. If this happens, a light on top will blink to summon an attendant. Again, don't leave, touch or take your eyes off the slot until the attendant arrives.

* After hitting a sizeable jackpot, most players simply walk away. Back-to-back jackpots on the same slot are possible, but unlikely.

If the slot isn't a linked progressive, try another few spins (no more than 10) to see whether the slot is still player friendly. If not, convert your winnings into big bills ($50, $100) except for the amount you intend to keep playing with. If you do this, you will have joined the ranks of the smart slot players who have beaten the house! If you don't, you'll be tempted to give it all back.

Walk away from a win at a linked progressive. Right after a hit, it resets to a relatively low amount.

Final tip. If you really hit it big, take a break from gambling —
at least for the rest of the day or evening. Give time for the adrenaline rush to wear off. Enjoy walking around the casino a winner!
Next day, start playing the way you normally do.

"Casino Quotes"

The first visit to a casino is like the first night of a honeymoon. The
expectation is high, but the results are usually disappointing.

What makes for a happy ending of some trips to a casino is the fact
that it has ended.

Do you know what an occasional jackpot win is? In boxing, they
call it the loser's share.

There are three kinds of slot players: the smart, the lucky, and the
majority.

Albert Einstein did a mathematical study of the European single-
zero roulette wheel. He concluded that the only way to beat the
game consistently is to steal chips when the croupier isn't looking.

Money doesn't really talk in a casino. It goes without saying.

One trouble with slot playing is that it starts out as fun.

You never know how short a month is until those casino ATM cash-
advance machine statements start coming in.

No win is enough to the gambler for whom enough it too little.

I enjoy reading fiction when I go into a casino. You know. Those
slot payout tables which show how much you can win.

The trouble with hitting the top jackpot is that it takes so long to
put it all back in.

THE QUARTER SLOT

The goal of the strategy below is to test as many 2-coin, 3-reel, single-payline, nonprogressive quarter slots as possible until you find the right slot to play. Sticking to 2-coin quarter slots will save you a lot of money

NOTE: Play no more than 3 coins at any quarter slot. If you play 4 to 5 coins, you'd get better odds playing one coin at a dollar slot.

To start:

1. Set a win goal per session ($25, $50, $?). The win amount you're going to cash in and take home. Size doesn't matter.

2. Buy 2 rolls of quarters ($20), or get coins directly from the slot. Put the coins into a coin cup. Don't play with coins lying in the tray.

3. Select a carousel or bank of 2-coin, 3-reel, single-payline, nonprogressive quarter slots *in an area of heavy traffic and visible from many directions on the casino floor!*

4. At slot #1, set a **test-spin** limit (4, 6, ? spins). Say 6 spins.

5. Insert **1 coin** at a time for these 6 spins.

6. If you lose 6 times in a row, go to slot #2 and start over (**1 coin**, 4, 6, ? spins).

7. If you get back just a few coins or credits, play them off — also **1 coin** at a time.

    EXCEPTIONS TO ONE-COIN LIMIT BET. Here are four suggested times to bet max coin: at an in-house progressive, at a linked progressive (Megabucks), during a hot streak, and at a slot with a *certified or guaranteed* payback.

8. If you start getting small but consistent wins or hit a hot streak, bet **2 coins**. And stay at that slot as long as it keeps paying. When it stops, set a losing-spin limit and move on.

Bet 1 coin to start, and set a firm test-spin limit!

SUGGESTED POST-WIN STRATEGY

The post-win strategy below was designed to be flexible. So feel free to change any figures or amounts to fit your particular bankroll or playing style. Do whatever works best for you.

SMALL TO MIDSIZE WINS ($50 to $400)

CAUTION: Don't get greedy! To greedy players, no win is ever enough. They want more. So they play and replay all coins and credits — and go from being a sure winner to a sure loser. To walk away a winner, do the following:

Just one More!

* Set aside the amount of the win goal (take-home money) you established for each session. Keep HALF of the rest of the win to shop, take in a show, pay trip expenses, etc. Try to keep at least half of all wins thereafter.

* Now, increase your bets to **2 coins** per spin. (Rule: double up only after a sizable win. Don't count the return of a few coins as a win.)

* Keep betting **2 coins** per spin as long as you're winning.

* The instant you sense or realize that you're no longer winning, set a firm losing-spin limit — no more than 5 to 10 spins!

* If you reach this losing-spin limit, stop playing! Not one extra pull. Setting losing-spin limits will keep you playing during a hot streak and will warn you when a cold streak has begun.

When no longer winning, set a firm losing-spin limit.
And stick to it!

BIG WIN (over $400)

IMPORTANT: After a big win, make sure that the figure in the WINNER PAID meter agrees with the figure shown for that particular win combination in the payout table. If it doesn't, the machine probably ran out of money or jammed. If this happens, the light on top of the machine will blink to summon an attendant. A figure like 3200 or 3300 will also appear in the credit meter. It's called a tilt code.

* Depending on the amount of the win, the payout may be made entirely by the slot (cash, voucher) or in part or full by an attendant.

* When part or all of the payout is to be made by an attendant, a light on top of the slot will blink, or the slot will make some kind of sound (loud ring or musical tone) to summon the attendant.

* Until the attendant arrives, don't touch, leave, or take your eyes off the slot for any reason. Big cash winners make big targets for the ever-present casino thieves.

* If the slot blacks out during a payout, it's probably due to a malfunction, a coin jam, or it simply ran out of coins. If this happens, a light on top will blink to summon an attendant. Again, don't leave, touch, or take your eyes off the slot until the attendant arrives.

* After hitting a sizeable jackpot, most players simply walk away. Back-to-back jackpots on the same slot are possible, but unlikely.

If the slot isn't a linked progressive, try another few spins (no more than 10) to see whether the slot is still player friendly. If not, convert your winnings into big bills ($50, $100), except for the amount you intend to keep playing with. If you do this, you will have joined the ranks of the smart slot players who have beaten the house! If you don't, you'll be tempted to give it all back.

Walk away from a win at a linked progressive. After one is hit, it resets to a relatively low amount.

Helpful hint. If you're doing well at the quarter slots, don't move up to a higher denomination slot. You increase your chances to win more if you do — and lose more if you don't.

But if you insist, move up only when you're ahead enough to justify the risk. Moving up with a shoestring bankroll is just asking for trouble. And if you do move up and find yourself becoming tense and sweating every spin of the reels, move back down. Winning a few $50 to $400 jackpots on the quarter slots is better than risking everything on an elusive, higher denomination jackpot.

Final tip. If you really hit it big, take a break from gambling — at least for the rest of the day or evening. Give time for the adrenaline rush to wear off. Enjoy walking around the casino a winner! Next day, start playing the way you normally do.

———————————— "Casino Quotes" ————————————

Casino gambling is not the world's oldest profession. Although the comparison has often been made.

One big slot loser couldn't take it any more. She went slot-raving mad.

Fun in a casino is like life insurance. The more you get, the more it costs.

Nothing new ever happens in a casino. Just the same old things. Only to different people.

Never bet on a sure thing unless you can afford to lose.

Casinos know you can't fool all of the people all of the time. But it isn't necessary. A majority will do.

A casino is glad that its patrons got what it takes.

Sign seen above a casino ATM: *THE LUCK STOPS HERE.*

THE NICKEL SLOT

The goal of the strategy below is to test as many 2- and 3-coin, 3-reel, single- and 3-payline, nonprogressive nickel slots as possible.

To start:

1. Get 5 rolls of nickels ($20), or get coins directly from the slot. Put the coins into a coin bucket. Don't play with coins lying in the tray.

2. Select a carousel or bank of 2- or 3-coin, 3-reel, single- and 3-payline, nonprogressive nickel slots *in an area of heavy traffic and visible from many directions of the casino floor.*

3. At slot #1, set a **test-spin** limit (5, 10, ? spins). Say 10 spins.

4. Insert **max coin** for these 10 spins. (Some players bet less than max coin — a judgment call.)

5. If you lose 10 times in a row, go to slot #2 and start over (**max coin**, 5, 10, ? spins).

6. If you get back a few coins, play them off. Cash out any credits and play the coins off.

7. If you start getting small but consistent wins or hit a hot streak, stay at that slot. Play as long as it keeps paying. When it stops paying, set a losing-spin limit and move on.

8. Otherwise, keep going from slot to slot until you've used up your alloted bankroll for the session. Then take a break (shop, stroll, lunch, etc.) until the next session.

SUGGESTED POST-WIN STRATEGY

The post-win strategy below was designed to be flexible. So feel free to change figures or amounts to fit your particular bankroll or playing style. Do whatever works best for you.

SMALL WIN - Up to 1000 Coins ($50)

Just one More!

CAUTION: Don't get greedy! To a greedy player, no win is ever enough. He always wants more. So he plays and replays all coins and credits and goes from being a sure winner to a sure loser. To walk away a winner, do the following:

Note: Many nickel slot players don't bother setting a win goal (take-home money). But it's still a good idea.

* After a small win, set a losing-spin limit — from 5 to 10 spins.

* If you reach this losing-spin limit, walk away.

* If you win again, stay at that slot, but set another losing-spin limit. Setting losing-spin limits keeps you playing during a hot streak and warns you when a cold streak has begun.

When no longer winning, set a firm losing-spin limit. And stick to it!

MIDSIZE TO BIG WIN (Over $50)

* A win over $50 is usually paid by voucher or in part or full by an attendant.

* When a payout is to be made by an attendant, a light on top of the slot will blink, or the slot will make some kind of noise (loud ring or musical tone) to summon the attendant.

* Until the attendant arrives, don't leave, touch, or take your eyes off the slot for any reason. Big winners make big targets for casino thieves.

* If a slot blacks out during a payout, it's probably due to a malfunction, coin jam, or it simply ran out of coins. If this happens, a light on top will blink to summon an attendant. Again, don't leave, touch, or take your eyes off the slot until the attendant arrives.

* After hitting a sizable jackpot, most players simply walk away. Back-to-back jackpots on the same slot are possible, but unlikely.

* You might, however, try another few spins (no more than 10) to see whether the slot is still player friendly. If not, cash everything in and take a break until the next session.

Final tip. If you really hit it big, take a break from gambling — at least for the rest of the day or evening. Give time for the adrenaline rush to wear off. Walk around the casino, luxuriating in the feeling of being a big winner. Tomorrow is another day.

———————— **"Casino Quotes"** ————————

The best way to judge a smart gambler is not by how much he wins, but by how much he keeps.

Everyone likes a good loser. Provided it's the other guy.

Slot hosts are ordered never to lie. Except when it's absolutely necessary.

Pit boss. A man who is never unintentionally rude.

One should always remember that what the casino gives away, it must first take away.

The reason you can't take it with you is that it goes before you do.

There's nothing more expensive than a free trip to Las Vegas .

First Things First

Captain to deckhand on a Mississippi riverboat casino: "If the boat hit a big object and started to sink, who would you save first? The young or the older women?"
Deckhand: "Me!"

A shapely Vegas chorus girl told her boss that she was quitting to marry a man she had met in the casino after the last show.
"That serious?" the boss asked.
"Absolutely," replied the girl. "I've always dreamed of marrying a man who's tall, dark, and has some."

A man returned from a weekend in Lake Tahoe. "How'd you make out at the slots?" asked a friend.
Man: "I lost all my money, except on the $5 slots."
Friend: "How's that?"
Man: "I didn't play them."

A poker-playing spiritualist needed another player for a Saturday night session and summoned the ghost of a departed companion. The ghost was delighted to sit in on the game. On the very first hand, he drew five beautiful hearts and bet his entire bankroll. Unfortunately, one of the live players had a full house and raked in the pot. Just another example of where the spirit was willing, but the flush was weak.

A lady slot player on a Mississippi riverboat casino became nervous when a sudden storm came up with wind and heavy waves, tossing the boat hither and yon. Going up to a security guard, she timidly asked, "Excuse me, sir. Do you have storms like this on the river very often?"
"No," said the guard. "Not very often."
"Do passengers ever get lost in the river during a storm like this?" she then asked.
"Oh, no lady," the guard answered reassuringly. "We always find them the next day."

A tourist goes into a restaurant of one of those posh European-themed casinos on the Las Vegas Strip. After being seated he asks the waiter, "Do you have a dinner for $20?"
Waiter: "Yes, sir, we do. Would you like it on white or rye?"

Etcetera

WHAT'S YOUR GOAL?

A. PLAYING SLOTS FOR FUN

Because casinos typically derive up to 70% of their income from slot machines and other electronic cash cows, they're constantly searching for new ways to offer their patrons a more fun-filled and exciting mix of gaming-entertainment experiences.

To meet the casinos' demands for something new and unique, slot makers gave birth to a dramatically new concept in slot gaming: *Slotertainment.* A term expressing the combining of traditional slot technology with entertainment features.

The result? A dizzying array of new machines with multigame touch screens, double bonuses, spinning wheels, encyclopedic pay tables, and dazzling colors and sound effects — all promising fast-paced fun and entertainment.

The new breed of slots was designed for those who play for the pure fun of the game — the slot FUNatics. Winning is not their main goal. If they lose, they don't care. One avid slot FUNatic exclaimed, "I play the new slots because I absolutely love them. If I win, great. If I lose, OK. I had fun."

It's true. Slots like Jeopardy, Wheel of Fortune, etc., are indeed fun and exciting to play. But all that glitters is not gold. The downside to these "fun" slots is that there's a lot of downtime associated with them. Meaning that to compensate for those spinning wheels and bonus games, the machines are programmed to keep more of your money (88% payback in some games).

Some of the games are silly, hard to understand, and costly to play! Here's what slot savant Frank Scoblete said about the new breed of multiline, multicoin slots: *"They're simply monsters that take your money at varying rates of speed. Play no machine that requires you to bet more than three coins for max play."* Sound advice.

91

B. PLAYING SLOTS TO WIN

There's no clear line between playing slots for fun and playing to win. But the number one reason people gamble is to win money. Period! No one's saying playing to win and having fun are mutually exclusive goals. But serious slot players play to win — not to be entertained. They may occasionally test drive the 5-reel, 5-to-20 payline slots for the novelty or out of curiosity. But they stick to the old favorites like IGT's Double Diamond, Wild Cherry, Sizzling 7s, and the ever-popular Red, White and Blue.

So let the thrill seekers plunk their money into the awesome Totem Poles, Treasure Tunnels, and TV game show slots. Stick to the 3-reel standards like those mentioned above. They may not be as exciting or as much fun to play, but they're better payers and you get better overall results.

"Casino Quotes"

What makes for a happy ending of some trips to a casino is the fact that it has ended.

Some psychologists say that it sometimes helps a marriage if you hit your wife. They may be right. Go to any major casino and you'll be amazed how many wives are sitting at tables saying, "Hit me again!"

A slot machine is sometimes like a small child. When it's good, it's very, very good. When it's bad, it's absolutely awful!

A positive attitude in a casino can be described as an illogical belief in the occurrence of the improbable.

Keeping your bets small is like the Chinese proverb: Falling hurts least those who fly low.

The casinos are determined to provide you with fun and entertainment even if it takes all the money you've got.

SOME NAMES AND ORIGINS

BEAT THE HOUSE. During the American colonial period, a "house" referred to a merchant's place of business. And a customer who could talk a merchant into giving him a better price could literally boast that he had "beaten the house." In today's usage, "house" refers to a place of business (*on the house*), a place of entertainment (*bring down the house*), and a gambling establishment.

BELLAGIO. Name of the ultra-luxe 1.8 billion dollar megaresort located on an 8.36 acre lake on the Las Vegas Strip. It was modeled after the tourist/resort town of Bellagio on the shore of Lake Como in northern Italy.

The management interprets Bellagio as Italian for "elegant relaxation." But the true derivation is from the Italian *bello* = nice, beautiful + *agio* = comfort.

BIG BERTHA. The name given to those giant dollar slot machines usually found near casino entrances — mostly as an advertising gimmick. In World War I, Big Bertha referred to the huge, long-range cannon used by the Germans to shell Paris. It was produced by the Krupp Works in Essen, Germany. The name was bestowed on the gun by the Krupp family in honor of Frau Bertha von Bohlen, head of the Krupp family. Today, the term is used to describe any tool or machine that is large or cumbersome. Hence, the Big Bertha slot machine.

BUGSY SIEGEL. Builder of the fabulous Flamingo Casino in Las Vegas. Born in 1906 in Brooklyn as Benjamin Siegel, he became a grammar-school dropout, petty thief, and a full-time mobster with his own gang. He was known for flying into an insane rage at the slightest provocation and would beat up or kill anyone who threat - ened or angered him in any way.

In the 1930's, insane asylums were called bughouses and their inmates bugs. Hence the nickname Bugsy. Siegel hated the name Bugsy and no one dared call him that to his face. "My friends call me Ben," he would caution. He was slain on June 20, 1947, by a 30-

30 carbine fired through a window of the rented Beverly Hills mansion of his girl friend, Virginia Hill, known in gangland by Siegel's pet name for her — Flamingo.

It was rumored that Siegel was downsized by East Coast mob investors, who suspected that he was using the massive cost overruns in the construction of the Flamingo to cheat them. The estimated cost was $1.5 million. Final cost was $6 million (about $22 million in 1999 dollars).

CASINO. The word "casino" in Italian means "little house." In Italy it is also used to refer to a gambling house and to a house of ill repute. Probably in the belief that the end result in either place is the same.

EDGE. A favorable margin or advantage. In a casino, the house edge refers to the small advantage (expressed in percentage) the casino has on every bet made. The higher the house edge, the lower the chances of winning.

A simple example. A and B decide to flip a coin. Each time A loses, he gives B $1.00. Each time A wins, B gives him 90 cents. So B has a 10% edge over A. This basically is how a casino stays in business. It takes in more money than it gives out. So it's easy to see that if you play long enough at a slot with a 92% payback (8% house edge) you'll eventually lose all your $$$.

In math parlance it's called a "negative expectation" game. You can occasionally win in a negative expectation game. But the longer you play, the more likely you're going to end up losing. The house always wins in the long run.

FOUR FLUSHER. Literally, a four flusher is a poker player who tries to pass off a four-card flush as a winning hand. Say a player is dealt three hearts, a spade and a club. He discards the spade and the club and draws two more cards, a heart and a diamond.

When he shows his hand, he calls it a flush and lays it down without spreading it out completely. The four hearts show, but just a corner of the diamond. He can get away with it if the players aren't alert. If he's questioned, he can pass it off as an honest mistake.

HOPPER. The part of the slot machine that holds and dispenses coins in single-file order through the machine's coin exit chute. From Old English *hopur*, a container for holding grain.

LAKE TAHOE. The lake was discovered in 1844 by soldier-surveyor, John C. Fremont, while on a government surveying mission. It was called by several names before finally being named Tahoe — from an Indian word meaning "big water."

LAS VEGAS. In the 1830's, Las Vegas served as a watering stop and comfort station for Spanish pack trains along the Old Spanish Trail (Santa Fe, NM, to Los Angeles). It was prized for its lush meadows, watered by a creek that rose from a series of bubbling springs. Las Vegas in Spanish means "the meadows." From the full Spanish place name *Nuestra Señora de los Dolores de Las Vegas* (Our Lady of Sorrows of the Meadows).

LOUD BOWL. The gambling industry's term for the steel tray at the bottom of the slot. The loud chain-like rattle of coins dropping into it is meant to remind everyone within earshot that money does indeed talk.

MEGA. In Greek, the word *megas* has two meanings: (1) *of large size* — as in megaresort and megajackpot. And (2) *one million.* Ed Rogich, an executive director of International Game Technology, maker of Megabucks, said that the original Megabucks machine was so named because the top prize was one million dollars. But with today's multimillion dollar jackpots, the first meaning of *large size* applies.

NAMBLING. Refers to gambling on the Internet. An acronym derived from **N**etwork g**AMBLING**. It brings gambling into the home via a computer screen. It's also called cyberspace gambling or cybergaming. One who gambles on the Internet is referred to as a **nambler** or **cybergamer**.

NEVADA. A Spanish word meaning "snow-capped." The name Spanish explorers gave to the snow-capped mountain ranges in the northern part of the state.

NUDGE SLOT. In a nudge slot, symbols move onto the payline from just above or just below. Example: in the Double Diamond slot, diamond symbols face up and down. If a diamond pointed down lands just above a payline, it drops down onto the payline. If a diamond pointed upwards lands just below the payline, it clicks up to the payline. Other nudge slots: Coral Reef, Saloon Bars, Jurassic Slots.

ODDS. A term that refers to the ratio of losses to wins. Example: in a game where the odds are expressed as 7 to 1, you have 7 chances to lose and 1 to win. In the October 1997 edition of the *Las Vegas Insider*, the odds of hitting the Wheel of Fortune progressive were given as 50,000,000 to 1. Megabucks has more reasonable odds: only 30,000,000 to 1.

ONE-ARMED BANDIT. In the Old West, two professional bandits were playing a rigged slot machine. After losing heavily, one crook said to the other, "Boy, with a machine like this, you don't need a gun to hold up anyone." "Yeah," replied the other crook. "And it only has one arm too!"

Here's a less colorful but more plausible origin. In the 1930's, a slot machine operator was arrested and tried for operating a gambling device.The judge, when sentencing the man, referred to the slot as a one-armed bandit. And the name stuck.

POKIE. The name given to the five-reel, multiline video slots that originated in Australia. They were called "pokies" since the first games in them were poker games. Poker is a five-card game, and the slot uses five reels.

RENO. The city of Reno was founded in 1868 during construction of the Central Pacific Railroad. It was named after Jesse Lee Reno, a Union general killed in the Civil War.

ROULETTE. The French word for wheel is "roue." By replacing the letter "e" with the letter "l" and adding the diminutive suffix "ette," you get "roulette" or "little wheel."

SLOT SLUDGE. The slimy grime that blackens your hands after 20 minutes or so of coin play.

VIDEO. In Latin, "video" is a verb form meaning "I see." Its use in a video game refers to the computer-generated images of cards, cartoon characters, ghostly hands, etc., a player sees displayed on a viewing screen. Example: Odyssey. The sound and musical effects produced by a slot are referred to as "audio." From the Latin "audio," meaning "I hear."

——————————"Casino Quotes"——————————

The new high-tech computerized slots do everything but think. They have a lot in common with many of those who play them.

Some people call it going home. Others call it returning from the scene of the crime.

A racehorse is the only creature that can take thousands of people for a ride at the same time.

Two senses are required in a casino: common and horse.

Gambling establishments are full of willing people. Those willing to lose and those willing to let them.

If profanity could affect the outcome of a slot game, there would be a lot fewer losers.

After winning at one of those 20-line, multicoin slots, you need the help of a slot host to explain why you won.

I played one of those slots that pay out in scrip. But no matter what I did, I always ended up getting the slot's equivalent of a "Dear John" letter.

No Fan of Frankie

A well-known comedian was once asked how much he would charge to appear with Frank Sinatra at one of his stage shows at the former Sands casino in Las Vegas. A price of $10,000 was named.

"Agreed," said the Sands agent. "Just one thing, however. You are not to mingle with Mr. Sinatra or any of his friends either before or after the show. Is that understood?"

"Absolutely," said the comedian. "And in that case, my fee will be only $5,000."

A Las Vegas schoolteacher *was taking her class through a local art museum. "With a single stroke of the brush," she said, "Leonardo da Vinci could change a smiling face into a frowning one." "That's nothing," said a little boy. "My father's a blackjack dealer at one of the casinos and he does it all the time."*

A lady tourist flags down *a bus on the Las Vegas Strip. When the door opens, she yells to the driver, "Does this bus go to the Liberace Museum?'*

Driver: "No, lady. It doesn't."

Tourist: "But you have a poster about the museum on the front of the bus."

Driver: "I know that, lady. There's also an ad for Boston baked beans on the back of the bus, but it doesn't go to Boston."

Driver on a Las Vegas *tour bus: "Immediately ahead of us, folks, are the Paris and Bellagio casinos. I'll stop in front of each a moment so that when you go home you can tell everyone that you stopped at the Bellagio and Paris casinos."*

Man to casino security *guard: "I've been robbed! Someone took my wallet!"*

Guard: "Did you feel a hand in your pocket?"

Man: "Yes, but I thought it was my wife's."

The slot hater: *"I hate slots. And I'm glad I hate 'em. 'Cause if I didn't hate 'em, I'd like 'em. And then I'd hate 'em.*

If Charles Dickens *lived today, he would never have written his immortal "A Christmas Carol." Tiny Tim would be covered by an HMO, Jacob Marley would be in Forest Lawn, and Scrooge would be a casino credit manager.*

PROBLEM GAMBLING

Gaming industry research shows that the primary reason people visit a casino is for the fun, excitement, and the anticipation of winning. They know their chances of losing are greater than of winning. But they accept the risk. To them, gambling is a form of benign entertainment — like going to a concert, movie, racetrack, etc. If they lose, OK. They got their money's worth of fun and excitement.

Unfortunately, a small minority of players lose control and become problem gamblers. Players who wager money they can't afford to lose (scared money) and to whom gambling is no longer a pleasant diversion, but an obsession.

According to Gambler's Anonymous, you may be a problem gambler if you answer yes to at least 7 of the following 18 questions:

1. Do you lose time from work or school due to gambling?
2. Does gambling make your home life unhappy?
3. Does gambling affect your reputation?
4. Do you ever feel remorse after gambling?
5. Do you ever gamble to get money with which to pay debts or to solve financial difficulties?
6. Does gambling cause a decrease in your ambition or efficiency?
7. After losing, do you feel you must return as soon as possible and win back your losses?
8. After a win, do you have a strong urge to return and win more?
9. Do you often gamble until your last dollar is gone?
10. Do you ever borrow to finance your gambling?
11. Do you ever sell anything to finance your gambling?
12. Do you ever gamble longer than you planned?
13. Do you ever gamble to escape worry or trouble?
14. Do you ever commit, or consider committing, an illegal act to finance your gambling?

15. Does gambling cause you to have difficulty sleeping?

16. Do arguments, disappointments, or frustrations create within you an urge to gamble?

17. Do you have an urge to celebrate good fortune by a few hours of gambling?

18. Do you ever consider self-destruction as a result of your gambling?

It's the sincerest hope of the publisher of this book that you never have the need to call one of the help line numbers. But if you do, don't hesitate to get the help you need.

The Confused Widow

A widow consulted a medium who put her in touch with her late husband.
"Henry," asked the woman. "Are you happy now?"
"I'm very happy," replied the spirit of Henry.
"Do they have casinos where you are?" the wife asked.
"Yes, they do," the spirit replied.
"Tell me, what is it like in Heaven?"
"Heaven?" exclaimed Henry. "What makes you think I'm in Heaven?"

A business executive rolls into his office after a big weekend in Atlantic City. "Get me my broker, Miss Smith."
Miss Smith: "Stock or pawn?"

Joe and Bill are conventioneers in Las Vegas.
Joe: "How's your luck?"
Bill: "Well, it's the same old story. One day I win. One day I lose."
Joe: "Then why don't you just play every other day?"

Elementary math teacher to gambler's son: "Johnny, tell the class how much is two and two."
Gambler's son: "Little Joe."

SUGGESTED READING

Break the One-Armed Bandits! by Frank Scoblete. From the birth of the slots in the 1890's to the creation of today's new smart machines, Scoblete explains how the machines work and how to beat them. You'll learn expert strategies and money-management systems that are geared to s-t-r-e-t-c-h-i-n-g your time at the machines while simultaneously reducing your risk. Everything you need to know to come home a winner.

178 pp., paperbound, $8.95 + $5.00 S&H. Paone Press, Box 610, Lynbrook, NY 11563. Credit Card Fax Orders: 1-516-596-0646. Credit Card Phone Orders: 1-800-944-0406.

Strictly Slots. *The magazine for slot and video poker players.* **Strictly Slots** identifies, analyzes and rates all of the new slot and video poker machines, sometimes before they even get to the casino! Monthly columns and departments include: The Aggravated Gambler, Frugal Tips, Perfectly Frank, Slot Club Spotlight, Slot Machine Highlights, Advanced Poker Strategy, High Limit, Casino Profiles, and much more! If you play slots, you'll love **Strictly Slots** magazine.

1 year (12 issues) $24 or 2 years (24 issues) Only $37!

For subscription information, call 1-800-969-0711 (Monday through Friday, 9 a.m. to 9 p.m. EST)

SLOT SAVVY

Here are the 15 most common mistakes slot players make. Check them out and see how many describe you:

1. Don't budget enough money to gamble with.

2. Take checkbook and credit cards to the casino.

3. Go over their budget and borrow from the casino's ATM.

4. Have no basic plan or playing strategy.

5. Bet max coin at slots with 5 reels and up to 20 paylines.

6. Don't know when to quit after a win.

7. Play wrong denomination slot for their budget.

8. Play with only the top jackpot as their goal.

9. Play maximum coins at all times.

10. Play off all winnings.

11. Stay too long at a cold slot.

12. Play slot at breakneck speed.

13. Play progressives.

14. Stay with just one or two machines.

15. Don't join the casino's slot club.

It's strange. Gambling was once termed a vice.
Now it's considered entertainment.
